iCanPlayMusic

SO-AFO-243

Guitar Player SONGBOOK

Over 90 rock hits and pop classics arranged for easy guitar, in standard notation with chord boxes, full lyrics, and suggested strumming patterns.

AMSCO PUBLICATIONS
part of the MUSIC SALES GROUP
New York/London/Paris/Sydney/Copenhagen/Berlin/Tokyo/Madrid

Exclusive Distributors:
Music Sales Corporation
257 Park Avenue South
New York, NY 10010 USA.

Music Sales Limited
14-15 Berners Street,
London W1T 3LJ, England.

Music Sales Pty Limited
20 Resolution Drive,
Caringbah, NSW 2229, Australia.

Order No. AM 994532
International Standard Book Number: 978-0-8256-3676-9

Cover design by Fresh Lemon
Project editors: Martin Shellard and David Bradley

Printed in the United States of America by
Vicks Lithograph and Printing Corporation

Contents

After Midnight

Words and Music by
J.J. Cale

Strumming style ↓ ↑↓ ↑↓ ↑↓↑
1 (&) a 2 & 3 (&) a 4 &

Moderate rock

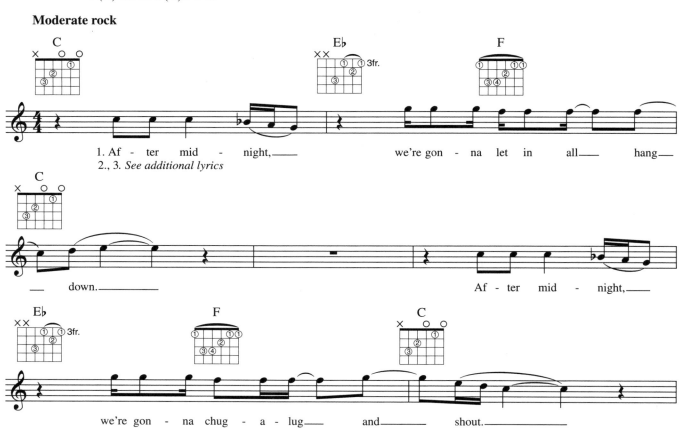

1. Af - ter mid - night, ____ we're gon - na let in all ___ hang ___
2., 3. *See additional lyrics*

___ down. _____ Af - ter mid - night, ____

we're gon - na chug - a - lug ___ and ___ shout. ___

We're gon - na stim - u - late ___ some ac - tion, ___

we're gon - na get some sat - is - fac - tion, we're gon - na find out ___ what it is all a -

bout. Af - ter mid - night, ____

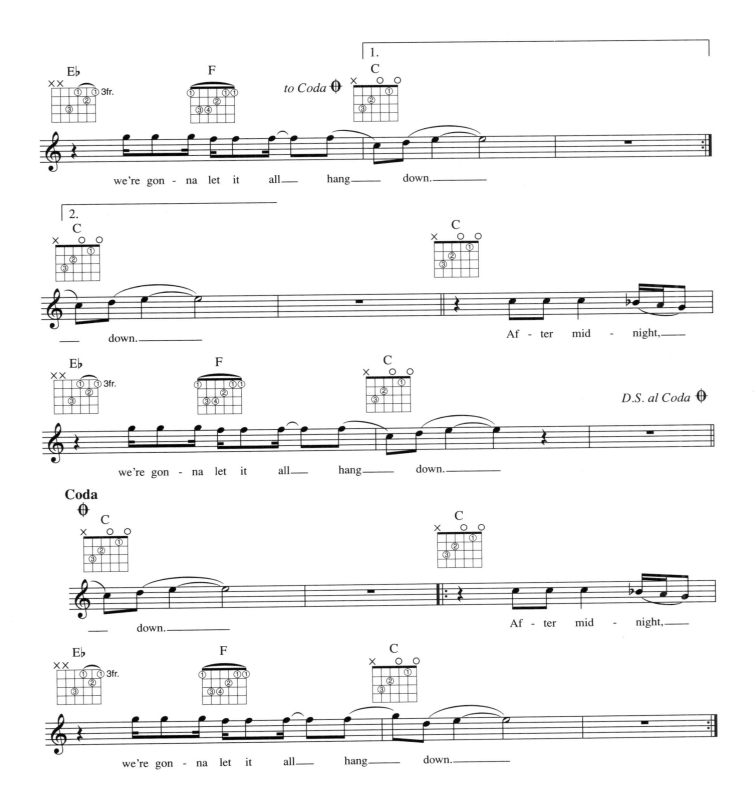

Additional lyrics

2., 3. After midnight, we're gonna shake your tambourine.
After midnight, it's all gonna be peaches and cream.
We're gonna cause talk and suspicion,
We're gonna give an exhibition,
We're gonna find out what it is all about.
After midnight, we're gonna let it all hang down.

All I Have To Do Is Dream

Words and Music by
Boudleaux Bryant

F♯m   B7   E   E7   A

an - y - time,   night or day.   On - ly trou - ble is,

G♯m   F♯7   B7

gee - whiz, I'm dream - ing my life____ a - way.   I____

E   C♯m   A   B   E   C♯m

need you so,   that I could die. I love you so,

A   B   E   C♯m   A   B

and that is why, when ev - er I want you____ all I have to do   is

E   C♯m   A   B   E   C♯m

dream,_____ dream, dream, dream,____ dream.____

A   B   E   C♯m   A   B

____ Dream,_____ dream, dream, dream.____

E   C♯m   A   B   *(repeat and fade)*

Dream,_____ dream, dream, dream.

7

Always On My Mind

Words and Music by
Wayne Thompson, Mark James and Johnny Christopher

D.C. al Coda

Tell___ me, tell me— that your sweet love— has-n't

died.— And give_____ me,— give me

one more chance to keep you sat-is fied,_____ I'll keep you sat-is-

Coda

You were al - ways on my mind,

you were al - ways on my_____ mind._____

Additional lyrics

2. Maybe I didn't hold you,
   All those lonely, lonely times.
   And I guess I never told you,
   I'm so happy that you're mine.
   Little things I should have said and done,
   I just never took the time.

3. *(Instrumental)*
   Little things I should have said and done,
   I just never took the time.

All I Wanna Do

Words and Music by
Sheryl Crow, Wyn Cooper, Kevin Gilbert, Bill Bottrell and David Baerwald

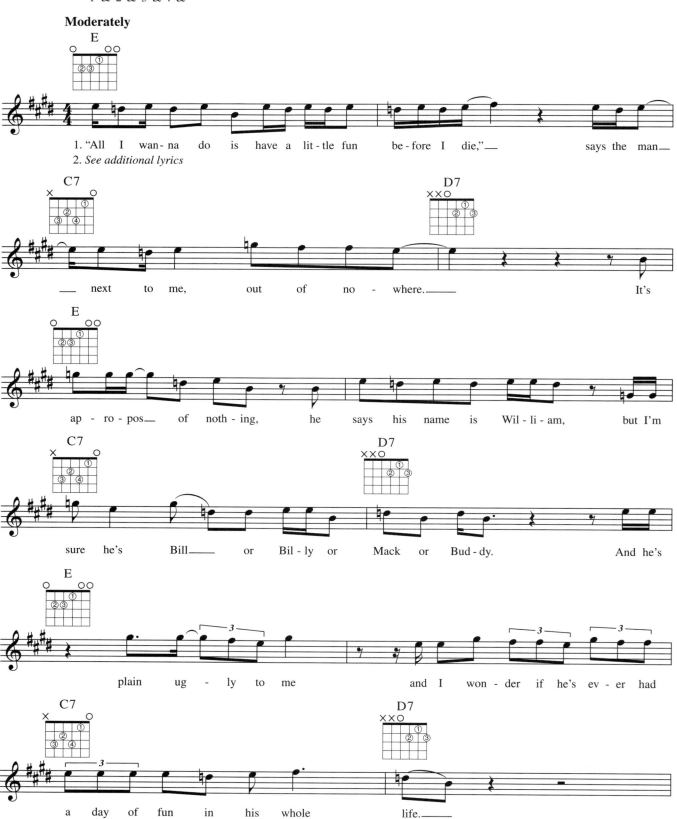

We are drink - ing beer at noon on Tues - day, in a

bar that fac - es a gi - ant car wash.—

And the good peo - ple of the world are wash - ing their cars— on their lunch break,

hos - ing and scrub - bing as best they can in skirts and suits.

They drive their shin - y Dat - suns and Bu - icks,

back to the phone com - pa - ny, the rec - ord store— too.

Well, they're— noth - ing like Bil - ly and me,— 'cos all I wan - na

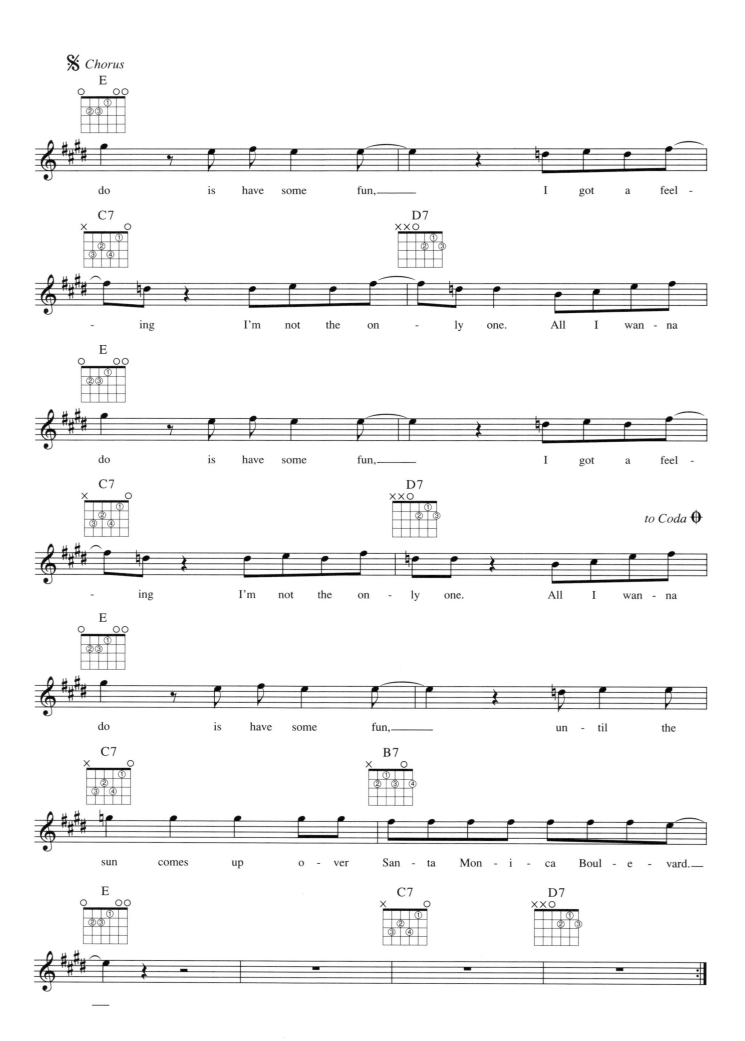

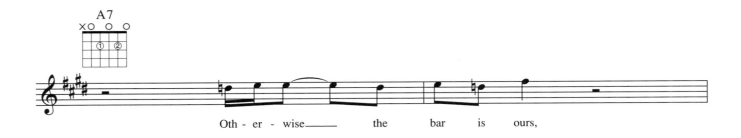

Oth - er - wise_____ the bar is ours,

the day and the night and the car wash too._____

And the match-es and the Buds and the clean and_____ dirt - y cars,

D.S. al Coda ⊕

the sun and the moon. But all I wan - na

Coda ⊕

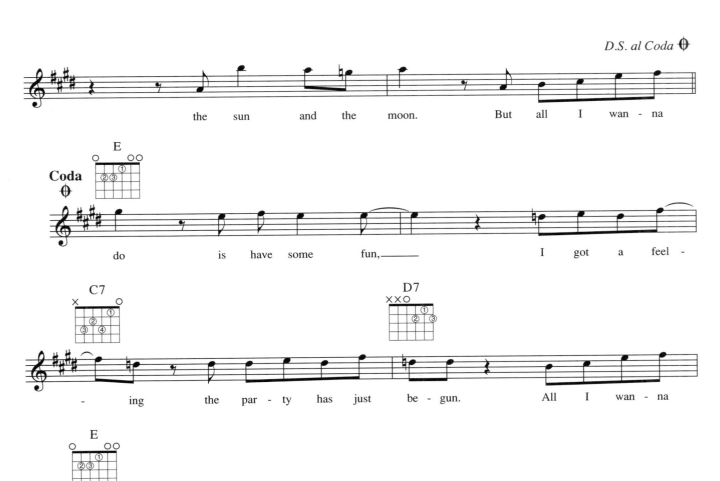

do is have some fun,_____ I got a feel -

- ing the par - ty has just be - gun. All I wan - na

do is have some fun._____ I won't tell_____

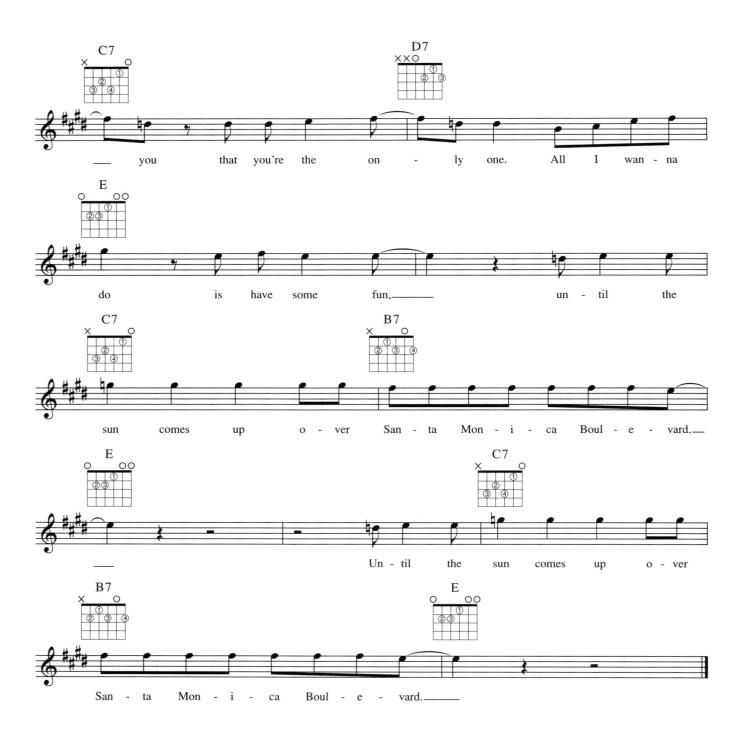

_____ you that you're the on - ly one. All I wan - na do is have some fun,_____ un - til the sun comes up o - ver San - ta Mon - i - ca Boul - e - vard.____ _____ Un - til the sun comes up o - ver San - ta Mon - i - ca Boul - e - vard._____

Additional lyrics

2. I like a good beer buzz early in the morning,
   And Billy likes to peel the labels from his bottles of Bud.
   He shreds them on the bar.
   Then he lights every match in an oversized pack,
   Letting each one burn down to his thick fingers,
   Before blowing and cursing them out.
   And he's watching the bottles of Bud
   As they spin on the floor,
   And a happy couple enters the bar,
   Dangerously close to one another;
   The bartender looks up from his want ads.

Angels

Words and Music by
Robert Peter Williams and Guy Chambers

she of - fers me— pro - tec - tion,— a lot of love and af - fec -

- tion, wheth - er I'm right or wrong. And down the wa - ter - fall,—

——————— wher - ev - er it— may take— me,— I know that life— won't break—

— me, when I come— to call. She won't for - sake—

— me,— I'm lov - ing an - gels in - stead.—

When I'm feel - ing weak and my pain— walks down— a one-

- way street.— I look a - bove and I know—

Amanda

Words and Music by
Tom Scholz

Additional lyrics

2. And I feel like today's the day,
   I'm lookin' for the words to say,
   Do you wanna be free, are you ready for me,
   To feel this way?
   I don't wanna lose you,
   So, it may be too soon, I know.
   The feeling takes so long to grow.
   If tell you today will you turn me away,
   And let me go?
   I don't wanna lose you.

Angel Eyes

Words and Music by
John Hiatt and Fred Koller

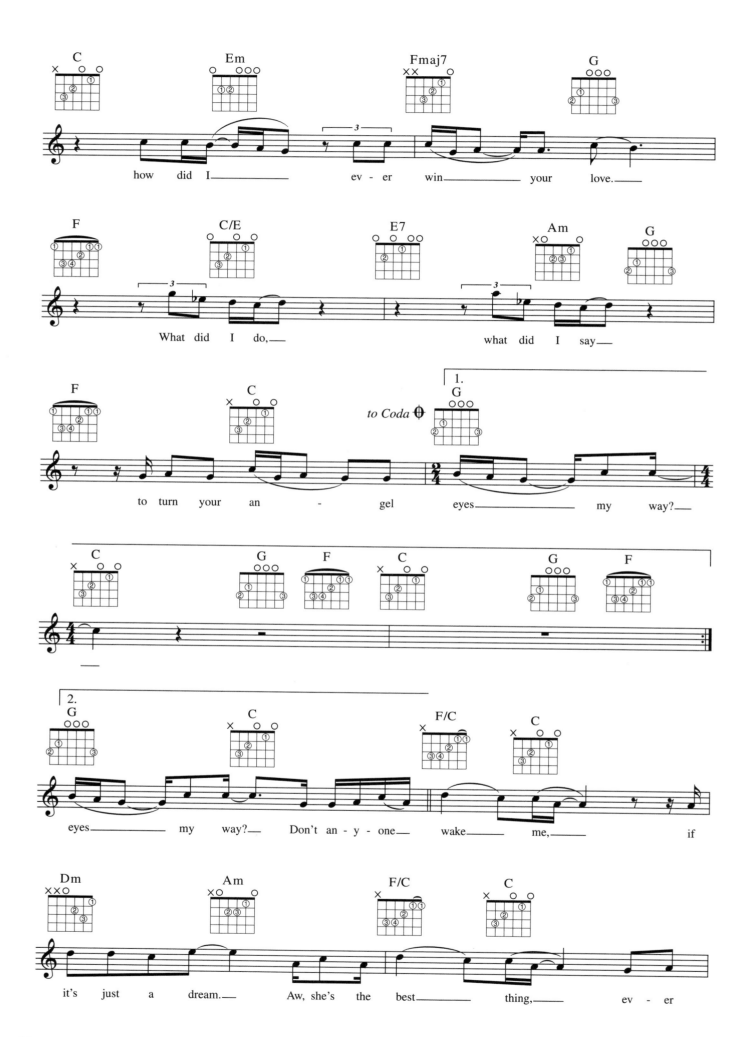

how did I _____ ev - er win _____ your love. _____

What did I do, ___ what did I say ___

to turn your an - gel eyes _____ my way?

eyes _____ my way? ___ Don't an - y - one ___ wake ___ me, ___ if

it's just a dream. ___ Aw, she's the best ___ thing, ___ ev - er

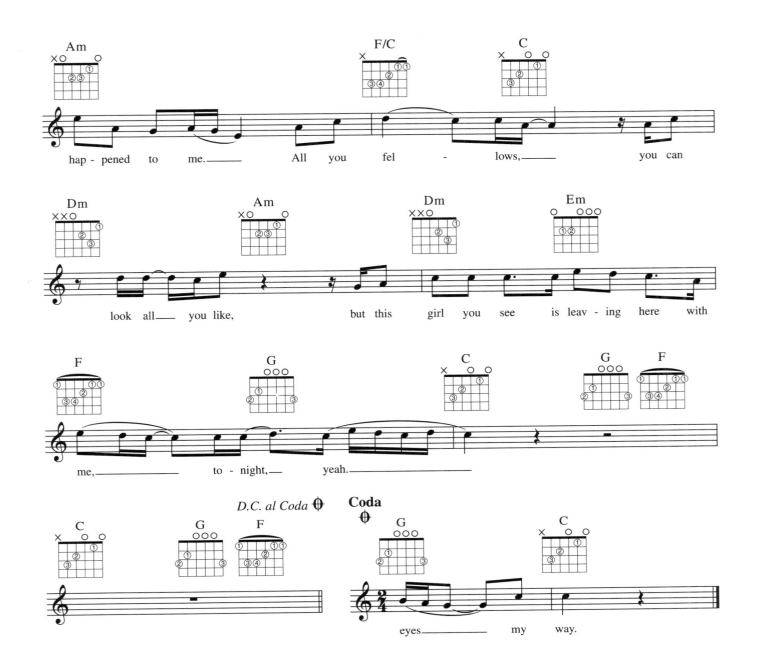

Any Way You Want It

Words and Music by
Steve Perry and Neal Schon

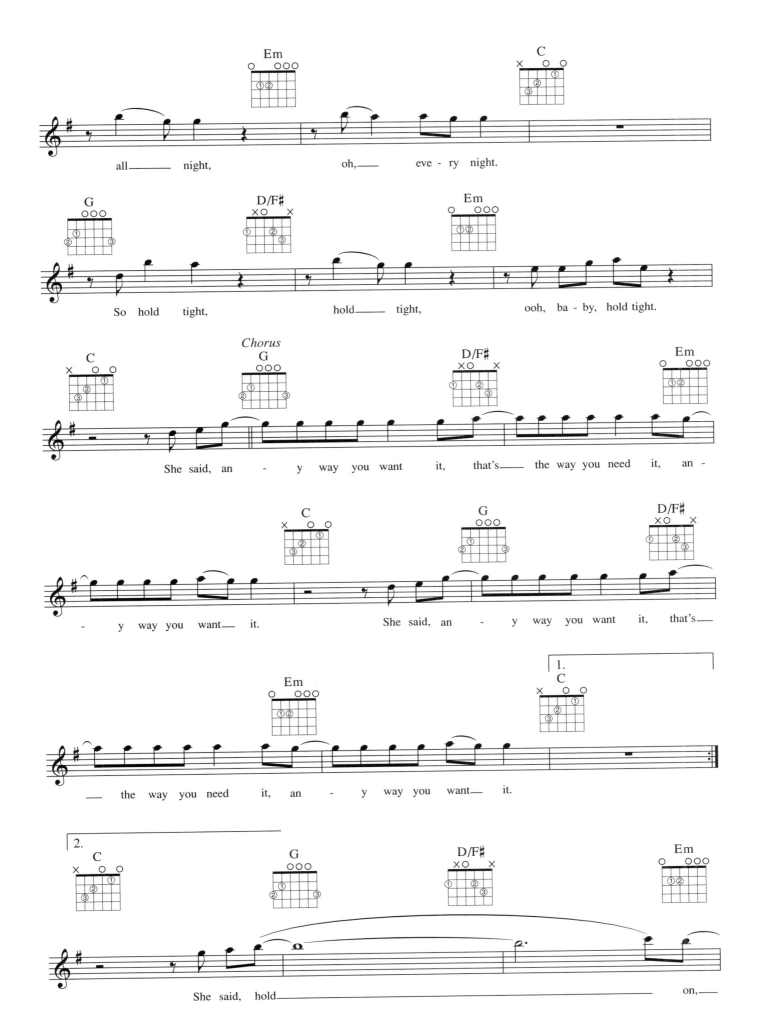

all_____ night,   oh,_____ eve - ry night.

So hold tight,   hold_____ tight,   ooh, ba - by, hold tight.

Chorus

She said, an - y way you want it, that's_____ the way you need it, an -

- y way you want_____ it.   She said, an - y way you want it, that's_____

1.

_____ the way you need it, an - y way you want_____ it.

2.

She said, hold_____ on,_____

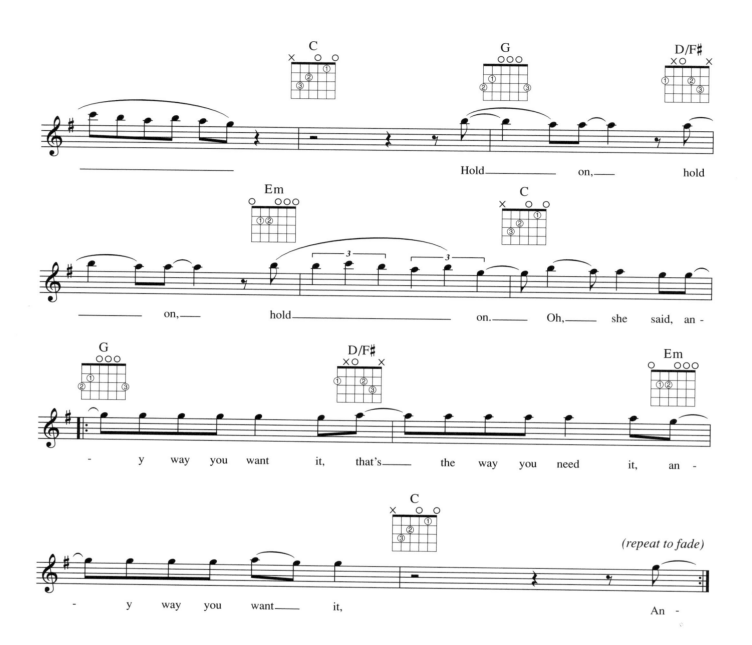

Additional lyrics

2. I was alone,
   I never knew
   What good love could do.
   Ooh, then we touched,
   Then we sang,
   About the lovin' things.
   Ooh, all night, all night,
   Oh, every night.
   So hold tight, hold tight,
   Ooh baby, hold tight.

Baby I Love Your Way

Words and Music by
Peter Frampton

Strumming style

1 & a (2) a & a 3 & a (4) a & a

Slowly

G · D/F♯ · Em

1. Shad-ows grow— so long— be-fore my eyes and they're
2., 3. *See additional lyrics*

C · F9

mov-ing a-cross the page.—

G · D/F♯ · Em

Sud-den-ly— the day— turns in-to night,— far a-

C · F9

way from the cit-y.— But

Bm7 · E7

don't hes-i-tate,— 'cos your

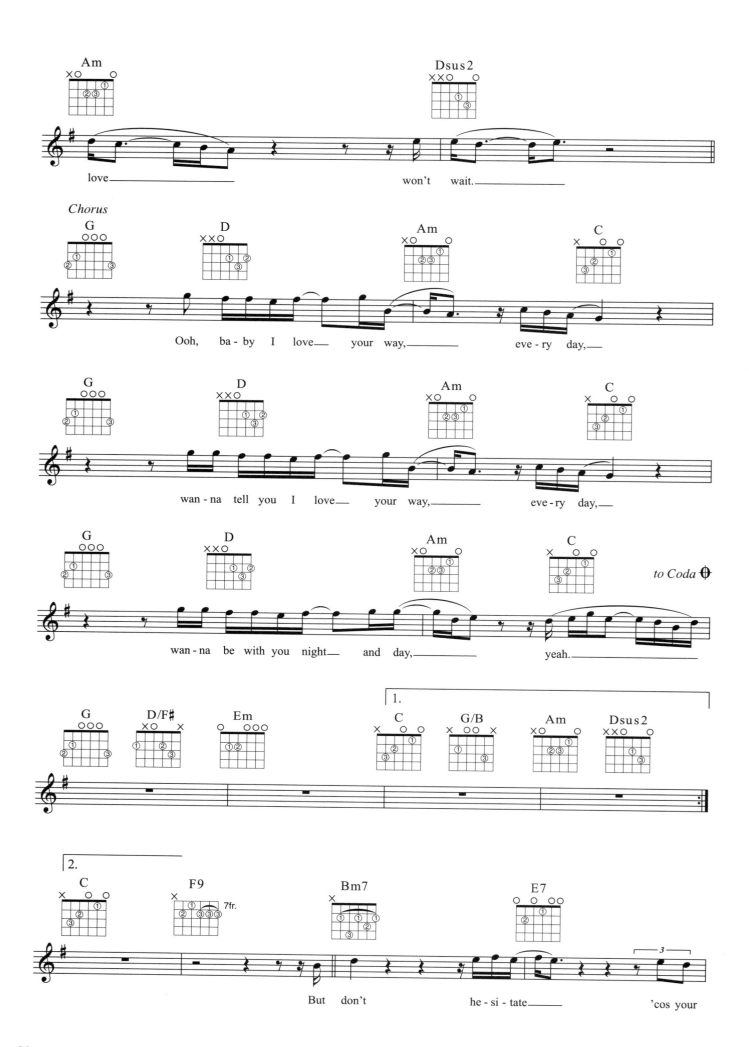

love_____ won't wait._____

Chorus

Ooh, ba - by I love___ your way,_____ eve - ry day,___

wan - na tell you I love___ your way,_____ eve - ry day,___

wan - na be with you night___ and day,_____ yeah._____

But don't he - si - tate_____ 'cos your

Additional lyrics

2. Moon appears to shine and light the sky,
   With the help of some fireflies.
   I wonder how they have the power shine, shine, shine,
   I can see them under the pines.
   But don't hesitate 'cos your love won't wait.

3. I can see the sunset in your eyes,
   Brown and gray and blue besides.
   Clouds are stalking islands in the sun,
   Wish I could buy one out of season.
   But don't hesitate 'cos your love won't wait.

Back In Black

Words and Music by
Angus Young, Malcolm Young and Brian Johnson

Strumming style ↓ ↓↑↓ ↓↑
Intro/Verse   1 (2) & a 3 (4) & a

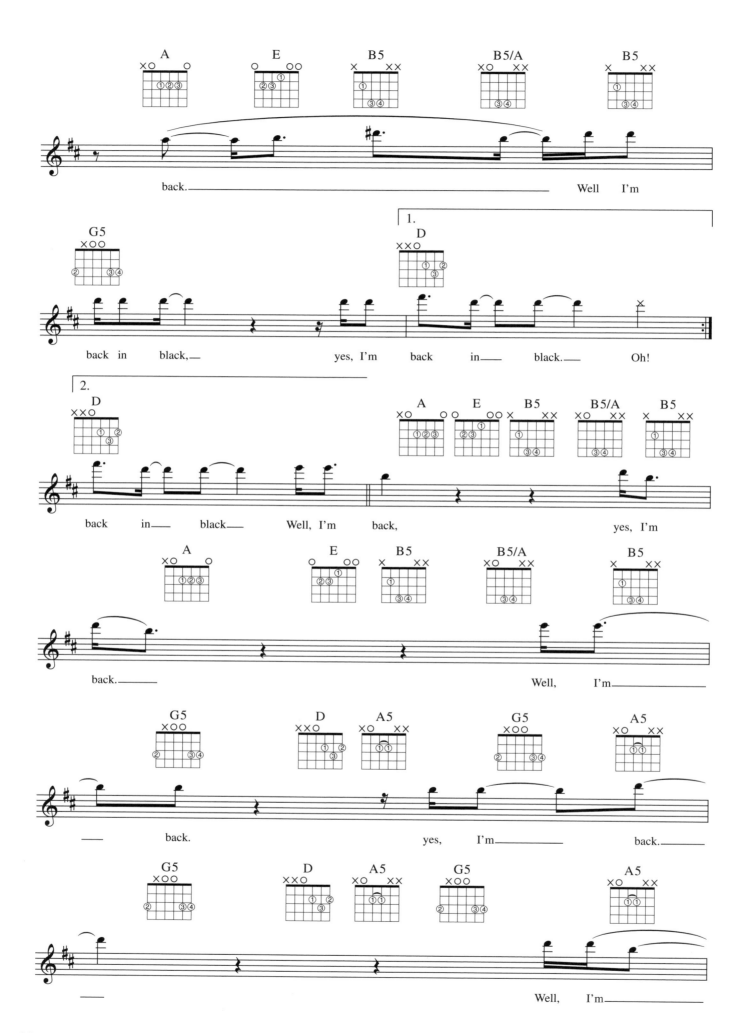

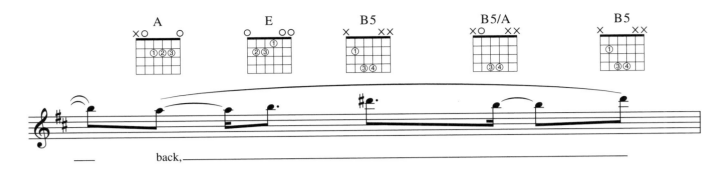

back,

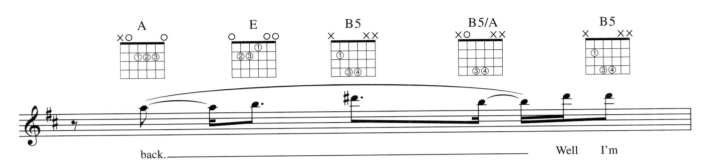

back.   Well   I'm

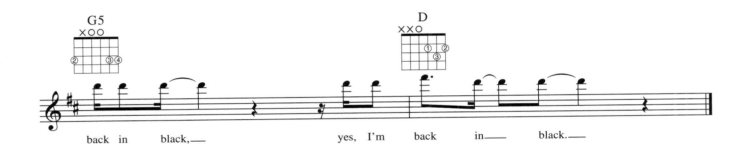

back in   black,   yes,   I'm   back   in   black.

Additional lyrics

2. Back in the back of a Cadillac,
    Number one with a bullet, I'm a power pack,
    Yes I'm in a bang with the gang,
    They gotta catch me if they want me to hang.
    'Cause I'm back on the track and I'm beatin' the flack,
    Nobody's gonna get me on another rap.
    So look at me now, I'm just makin' my play,
    Don't try to push your luck, just get out of my way.
    'Cause I'm back, yes I'm back...

Bad Day

Words and Music by
Daniel Powter

Strumming style ↓ ↑ ↓ ↓ ↑ ↓ ↑ ↓ ↓ ↑

1 & 2 & a 3 & 4 & a

Slowly

E   Asus2   B

1. Where is the mo - ment we need - ed the most?____

2., 3. *See additional lyrics*

E   Asus2

You kick up the leaves____ and the ma - gic is lost.____

B   C♯m   E/B

They tell me your blue____ skies turned____ to gray,____

A   E/G♯

they tell me your pas - sion's gone____ a - way,____

F♯m7   1. B

____ and I don't need____ no car - ryin' on____

2. - 3. B   *Chorus* E   Asus2

____ 'Cause you had a bad day, you've tak - en one down, you sing a sad

*Optional tune down 1/2 step

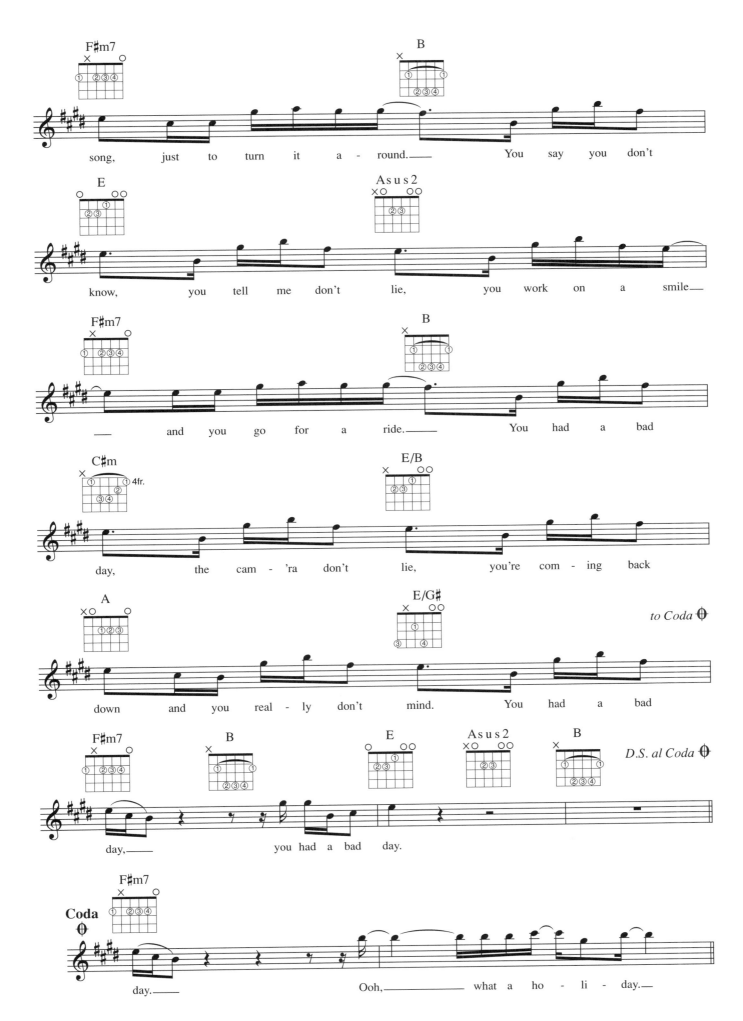

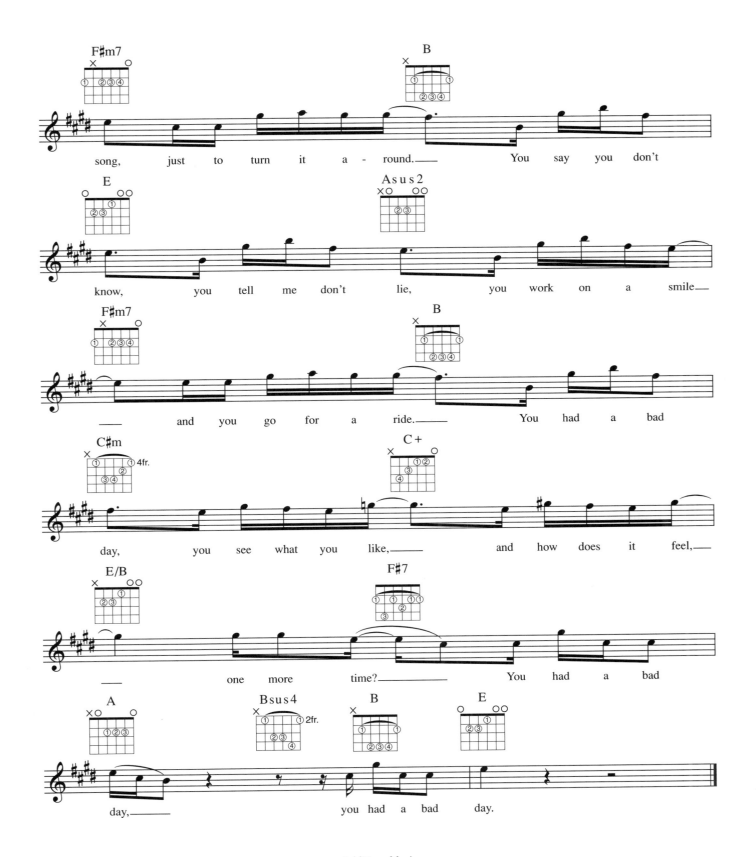

Additional lyrics

2. You stand in the line just to hit a new low,
   You're faking a smike with the coffee to go,
   You tell me your life's been way off line,
   You're falling to pieces every time,
   And I don't need no carryin' on.

3. (𝄋)Well, you need a blue-sky holiday,
   The point is, they laugh at what you say,
   And I don't need no carryin' on.

Because

Words and Music by
Dave Clark

Blitzkrieg Bop

Words and Music by
Jeffrey Hyman, John Cummings, Douglas Colvin and Thomas Erdelyi

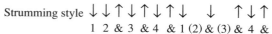

Blue Suede Shoes

Words and Music by
Carl Lee Perkins

Coda

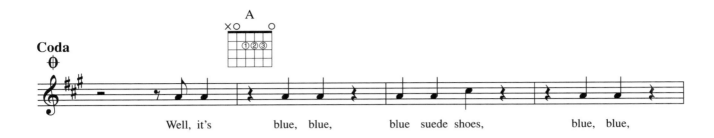

Well, it's blue, blue, blue suede shoes, blue, blue,

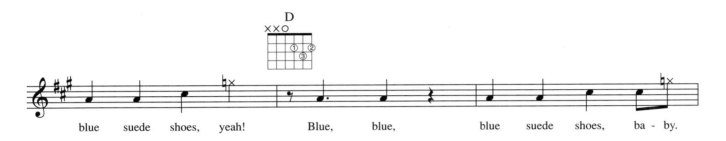

blue suede shoes, yeah! Blue, blue, blue suede shoes, ba - by.

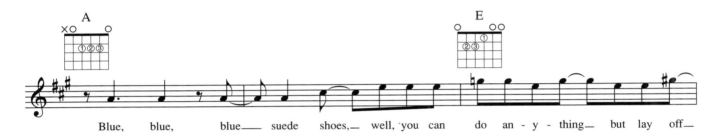

Blue, blue, blue— suede shoes,— well, you can do an - y - thing— but lay off—

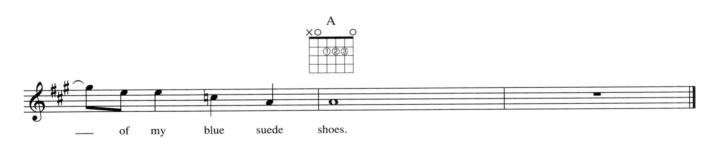

— of my blue suede shoes.

Additional lyrics

2. Well, you can knock me down,
Step in my face,
Slander my name all over the place,
Do anything that you wanna do,
But uh-uh honey, lay off of them shoes.
Chorus

3. Well, you can burn my house,
Steal my car,
Drink my liquor from an old fruitjar,
Do anything that you wanna do,
But uh-uh honey, lay off of my shoes.
Chorus

4. Well, it's a-one for the money,
Two for the show,
Three to get ready,
Now go, go, go.
Chorus

Brown Eyed Girl

Words and Music by
Van Morrison

Additional lyrics

2. And whatever happened,
   To Tuesday and so slow?
   Going down the old mine,
   With a transistor radio.
   Standing in the sunlight laughing,
   Hiding behind a rainbow's wall.
   Slipping and sliding,
   All along the water fall
   With you, my brown eyed girl.
   You, my brown eyed girl.

3. So hard to find my way,
   Now that I'm all on my own.
   I saw you just the other day;
   My, how you have grown.
   Cast my memory back there,
   Lord, sometimes I'm overcome thinking 'bout
   Laughing and a-running, hey, hey,
   Behind the stadium
   With you, my brown eyed girl.
   You, my brown eyed girl.

Buffalo Soldier

Words and Music by
Bob Marley and Noel Williams

※ *See additional lyrics*

D.S. al Fine

Additional lyrics

 %{ Buffalo soldier in the war for America,
     Buffalo soldier, dreadlock rasta,
     Fighting on arrival, fighting for survival,
     Driven from the mainland
     To the heart of the Caribbean.

Bye Bye Love

Words and Music by
Boudleaux Byrant

Strumming style ↓ ↓ ↑ ↓ ↑ ↓ ↑
1 2 & 3 & 4 &

Moderately fast

Bye, bye___ love,___ bye, bye___ hap - pi - ness,___

hel - lo lone - li - ness,___ I think I'm a - gon - na cry,___

Bye, bye___ love,___ bye, bye___ sweet___ ca - ress,___

hel - lo emp - ti - ness,___ I feel like I___ could die.___ Bye, bye___

to Coda ✛

___ my love,___ good - bye.___

1. There goes my
2. *See additional lyrics*

ba - by___ with some - one new.___ She___ sure___ looks

48

Additional lyrics

2. I'm a-through with romance,
   I'm a-through with love,
   I'm through with a-countin'
   The stars above.
   And here's reason
   That I'm so free:
   My lovin' baby
   Is a-through with me.

Brain Damage

Words and Music by
Roger Waters

Verse arpeggio   r m i   m T r m i   m T
1 & a (2) a & 3 & a (4) a &

Chorus strumming style ↓ ↓   ↑ ↓ ↑ ↓ ↑   ↑
1 2 (&) a 3 & 4 a (&) a

Slowly

Verse

D   G7

1. The lu - na - tic   is on the grass,___
2., 3. *See additional lyrics*

D   G7

the lu - na - tic   is on the grass,___

D   E/D

re - mem - ber - ing games   and dai - sy chains___ and laughs,___

to Coda ⊕

A7   D   Dsus2   D7

got to keep___ the loon - ies on___ the path.___

Chorus

G   A

And if the dam___ breaks o - pen man - y years too soon,___   and

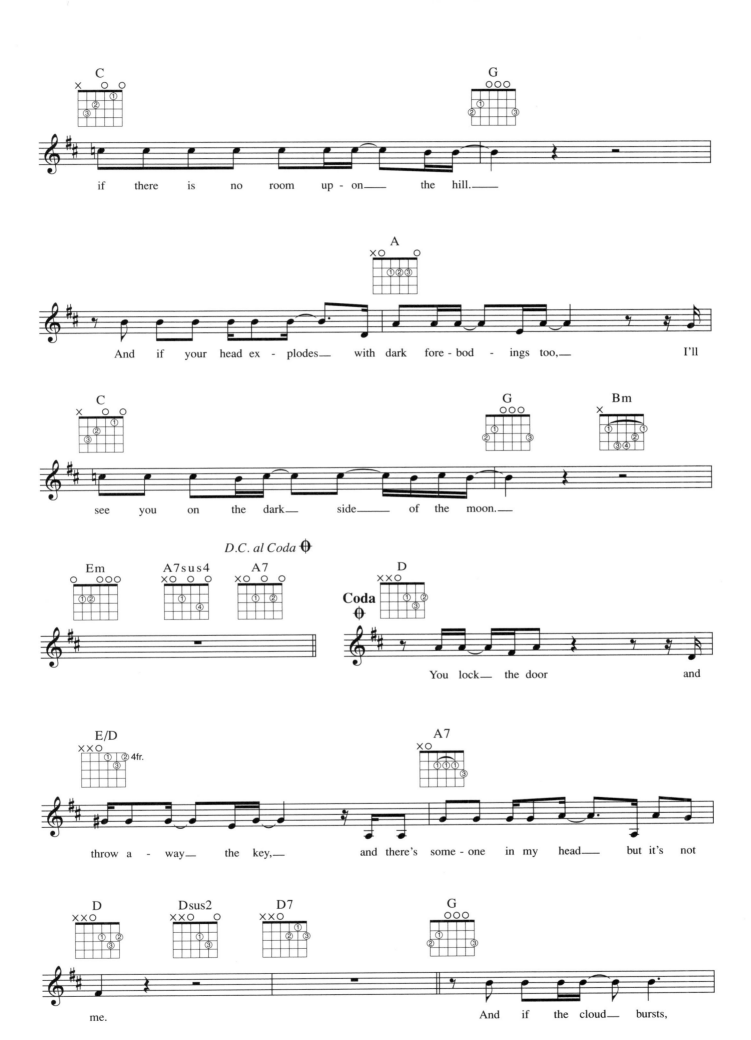

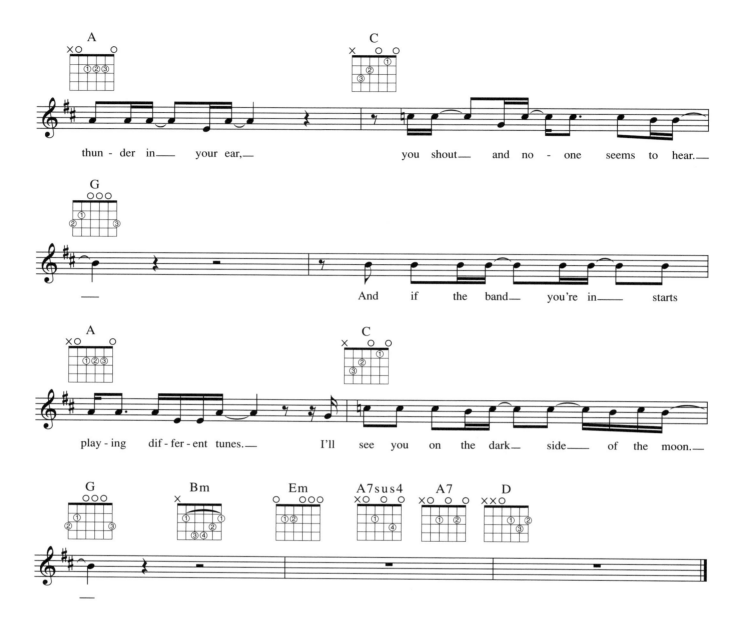

thun - der in___ your ear,___ you shout___ and no - one seems to hear.___

___ And if the band___ you're in___ starts

play - ing dif - fer - ent tunes.___ I'll see you on the dark___ side___ of the moon.___

___

Additional lyrics

2. The lunatic is in the hall,
   The lunatics are in my home,
   The paper holds their folded faces to the floor,
   And every day the paperboy brings more.

3. The lunatic is in my head,
   The lunatic is in my head,
   You raise the blade, you make the change,
   You rearrange me 'til I'm sane.

Complicated

Words and Music by
Lauren Christy, Graham Edwards, Scott Spock and Avril Lavigne

Strumming style ↓ ↑ ↓ ↓ ↑ ↓ ↑ ↓ ↓ ↑
1 & 2 & a 3 & 4 & a

Moderately

F   Dm

1. Chill out, what you yel - ling for? Lay back, it's all be done be - fore
2. *See additional lyrics*

Bbsus2   C

and if you could on - ly __ let it be, __ you would see. __

F   Dm

I like you the way __ you are when we're driv - ing in __ your car,

Bbsus2   C

and you're talk - ing to __ me, one on one. __ But you be - come __

Bbsus2   Dm

some - bo - dy else 'round eve - ry - one else, you're watch - ing your back, like you can't re - lax.

Bbsus2   C

Try - in' to be cool, you look like a fool to me. __ Tell __ me,

Coda

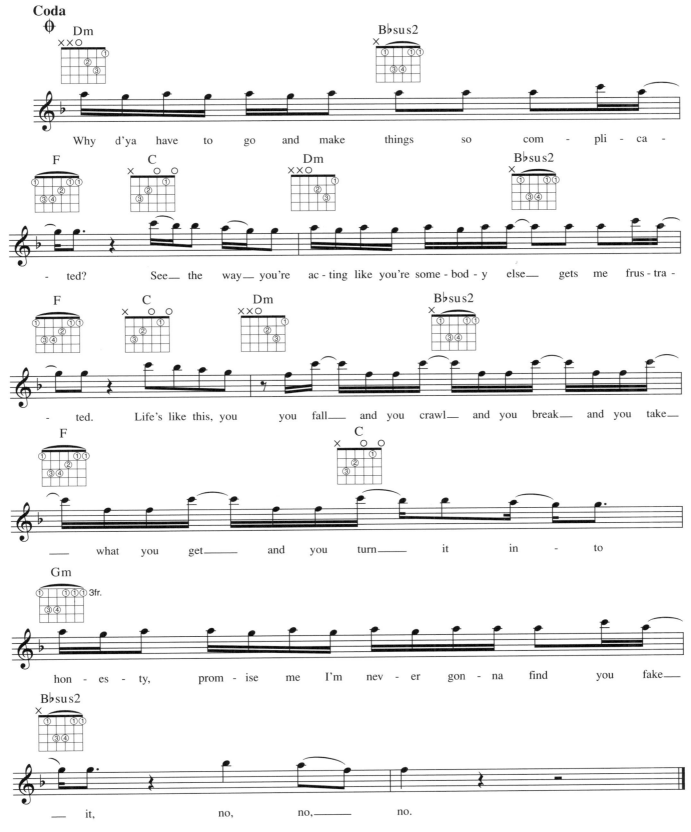

Why d'ya have to go and make things so com - pli - ca -

- ted? See— the way— you're ac - ting like you're some - bod - y else— gets me frus - tra -

- ted. Life's like this, you you fall— and you crawl— and you break— and you take—

— what you get— and you turn— it in - to

hon - es - ty, prom - ise me I'm nev - er gon - na find you fake—

— it, no, no,— no.

Additional lyrics

2. You come over unannounced,
   Dressed up like you're something else.
   Where you are and where it's at,
   You see, you're making me,
   Laugh out, when you strike your pose.
   Take off all your preppy clothes,
   You know, you're not fooling anyone,
   When you become...

Can't Fight This Feeling

Words and Music by
Kevin Cronin

Strumming style ↓ ↑ ↓ ↑ ↓ ↑ ↓ ↑
1 & 2 & 3 & 4 &

Moderate rock

A · Asus2 · A

1. I can't fight— this feel-ing an-y long- er,   and

Bm · F# · Esus4 · E

yet I'm still— a-fraid——— to let it flow.——— What

A · E/G# · G · F#

start-ed out— as friend-ship has grown— strong- er,——— I on-ly

Bm · A/C# · D · Esus4 · E

wish I had— had strength— to let it show.——— 2. I

A · E/G# · F#m7

tell my-self— that I can't hold out— for-ev- er.   I

Bm · F# · Esus4 · E

say there is— no rea-son for— my fear.——— 'Cause

I feel so___ se-cure___ when we're___ to-geth - er,_____ you

give my life___ di-rec - tion,___ you make eve - ry-thing___ so___

___ clear._____ And ev-en as___ I wan-der, I'm

keep-ing you___ in sight. You're a can-dle in___ the win - dow on a cold,___

___ dark win-ter's night,___ and I'm get-ting clos - er than I___

___ ev - er thought___ I___ might._____

And I___ can't fight___ this feel - ing an - y-more,___

Crazy Little Thing Called Love

Words and Music by
Freddie Mercury

Dear Mr. Fantasy

Words and Music by
Steve Winwood, Chris Wood and Jim Capaldi

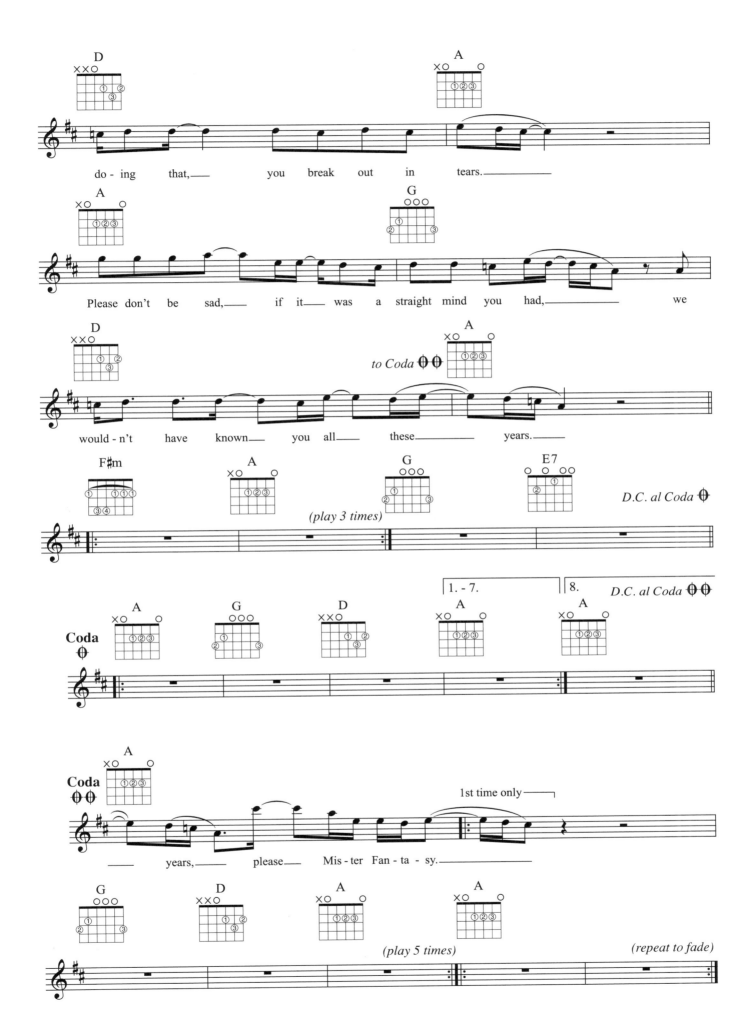

Doctor My Eyes

Words and Music by
Jackson Browne

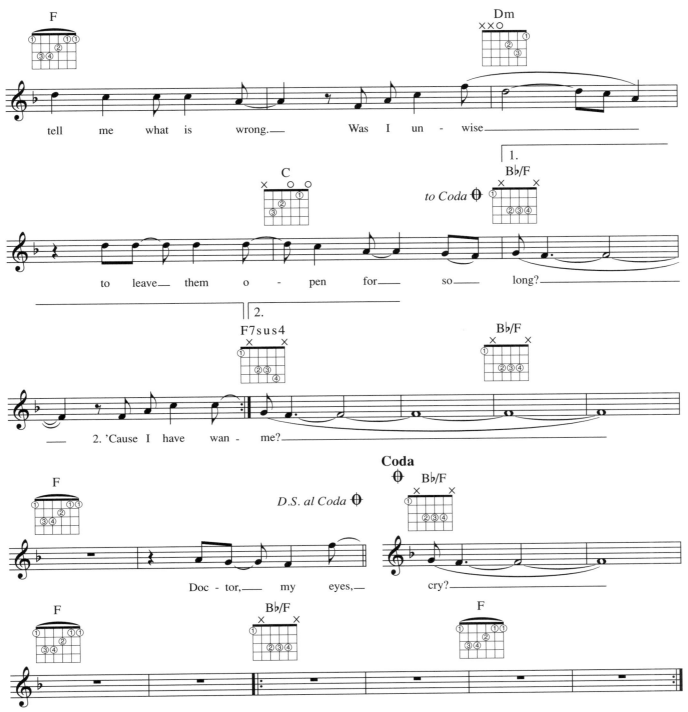

Additional lyrics

2. 'Cause I have wandered through this world,
And as each moment has unfurled,
I've been waiting to awaken from these dreams.
People go just where they will,
I never noticed them until I got this feeling
That it's later than it seems.

Chorus:
Doctor, my eyes,
Tell me what you see,
I hear their cries,
Just say if it's too late for me.

𝄋 Chorus:
Doctor, my eyes,
They cannot see the sky.
Is this the prize
For having learned how not to cry?

Don't Let Me Be Misunderstood

Words and Music by
Bennie Benjamin, Sol Marcus and Gloria Caldwell

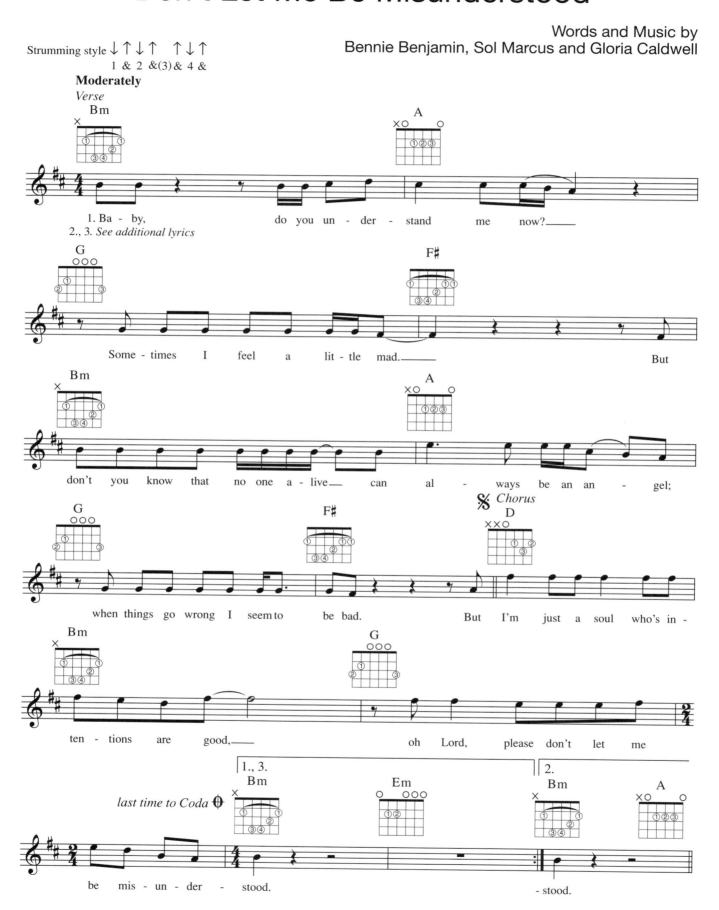

Additional lyrics

2. Baby, sometimes I'm so carefree,
   With a joy that's hard to hide.
   And sometimes it seems that all I have do is worry,
   Then you're bound to see my other side.

3. Oh, oh baby, don't you know I'm human?
   Have thoughts like any other one.
   Sometimes I find myself alone, regretting,
   Some foolish thing, some little sinful thing I've done.

Crazy On You

Words and Music by
Ann Wilson, Nancy Wilson and Roger Fisher

but go cra - zy on you, cra - zy on you,
Lem- me go cra - zy on you,

lem - me go cra - zy, cra - zy on you. 2. My

2. Wild man's world is

cry - ing in pain, what you gon - na do when eve - ry - bod - y's in - sane?

So a - fraid of one who's so a - fraid of you, what you

gon - na do?

Additional lyrics

2. My love is the evening breeze touching your skin,
   The gentle sweet singing of leaves in the wind,
   The whisper that calls after you in the night,
   And kisses your ear in the early light,
   And you don't need to wonder, you're doing fine,
   It's mine, love, the pleasure's mine.

3. I was a willow last night in my dream,
   I bent down over a clear running stream.
   I sang you the song that I heard up above,
   And you kept me alive with your sweet, flowing love.

Don't Stop Believin'

Words and Music by
Steve Perry, Neal Schon and Jonathan Cain

Strumming style ↓ ↑ ↓ ↑ ↓ ↑ ↓ ↑

1 & 2 & 3 & 4 &

Additional lyrics

2. Working hard to get my fill,
   Everybody wants a thrill,
   Paying anything to roll the dice
   Just one more time.
   Some will win, some will lose,
   Some are born to sing the blues.
   Oh, the movie never ends,
   It goes on and on and on and on.

(Everything I Do) I Do It For You

from the Motion Picture *ROBIN HOOD: PRINCE OF THIEVES*

Words and Music by
Bryan Adams, R.J. Lange and Michael Kamen

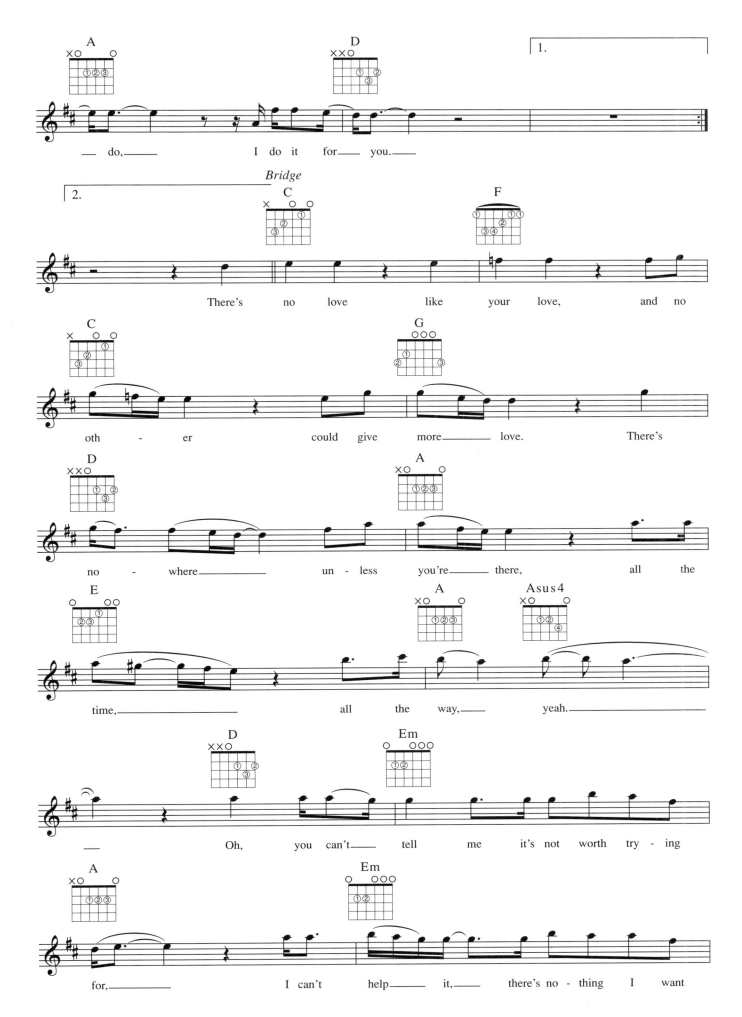

more.———— Yeah,— I would fight— for you,——— I'd

lie——— for you,——— walk the wire—— for you,——— yeah, I'd

die for— you.——— You know it's

true, eve - ry - thing I——— do,——— oh,———————

— I do it for——— you.

Additional lyrics

2. Look into your heart, you will find
   There's nothing there to hide.
   Take me as I am, take my life;
   I would give it all, I would sacrifice.
   Don't tell me it's not worth fighting for,
   I can't help it, there's nothing I want more.
   You know it's true,
   Everything I do, I do it for you.

Everyday Is A Winding Road

Words and Music by
Sheryl Crow, Brian MacLeod and Jeff Trott

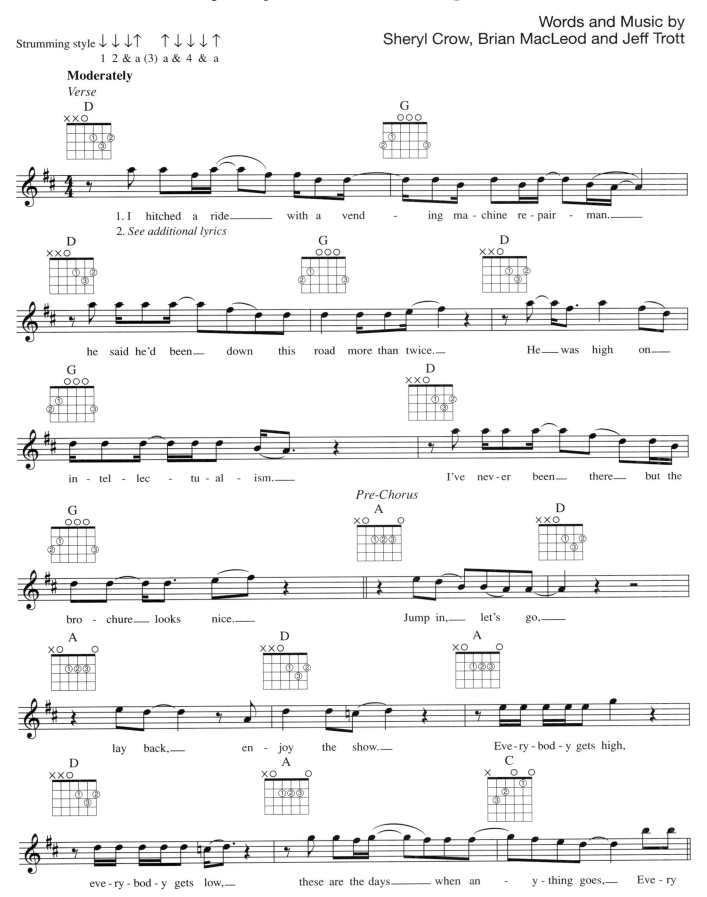

Additional lyrics

2. He's got a daughter he calls Easter,
   She was born on a Tuesday night.
   I'm just wondering why I feel so all alone,
   Why I'm a stranger in my own life.

Everywhere

Words and Music by
John Shanks and Michelle Branch

Strumming style ↓ ↑ ↓ ↓ ↑ ↓ ↑ ↓ ↓ ↑
                 1 & 2 & a 3 & 4 & a

Picking style T i mi T i m i T
               1 & 2 & 3 & a (4) a &

Moderately

Am   C   G

1. Turn it in-side out___ so I___ can see,___
2. *See additional lyrics*

Am   C   G

the part of you that's drift - ing o - ver me.___ And when I wake___ you're___

D/F#   G

___ you're nev - er there,_____ and when I sleep___ you're___

| 1.

Am   D9/F#   G

___ you're eve - ry - where,___ you're eve - ry - where.___

|| 2.

Am   C   G   G

'Cause you're

*Optional capo 1st fret

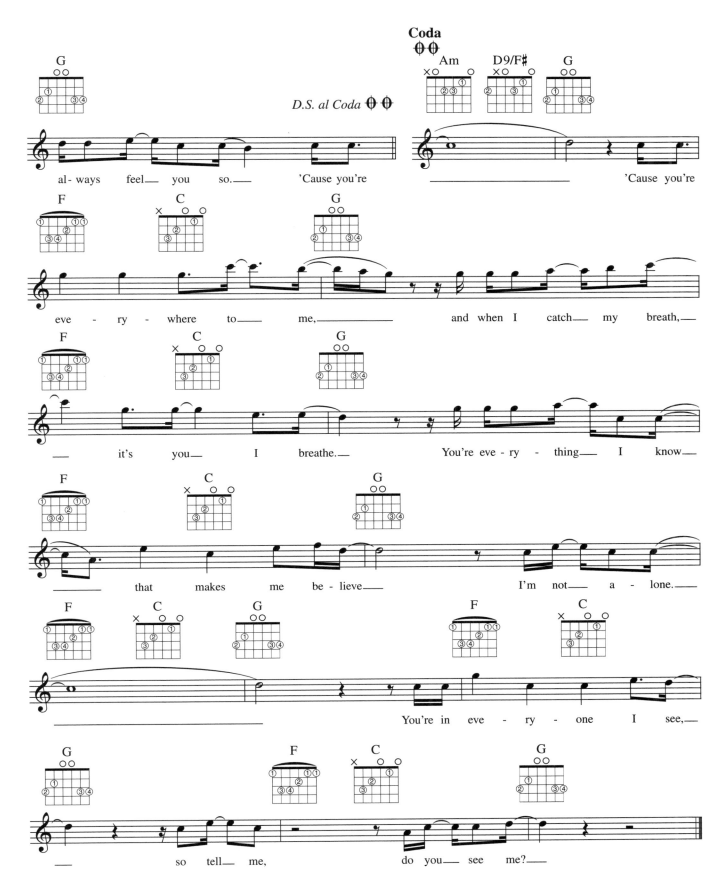

Faith

Words and Music by
George Michael

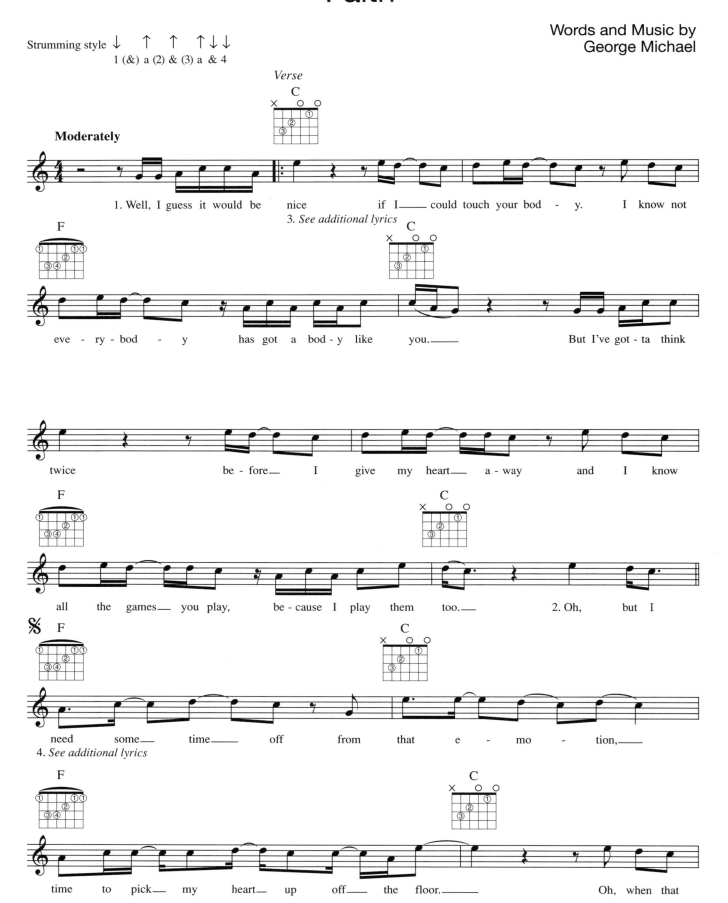

Strumming style ↓ ↑ ↑ ↑↓↓
1 (&) a (2) & (3) a & 4

Verse

Moderately

1. Well, I guess it would be nice if I____ could touch your bod - y. I know not

3. *See additional lyrics*

eve - ry - bod - y has got a bod - y like you.____ But I've got - ta think

twice be - fore____ I give my heart____ a - way and I know

all the games____ you play, be - cause I play them too.____ 2. Oh, but I

need some____ time____ off from that e - mo - tion,____

4. *See additional lyrics*

time to pick____ my heart____ up off____ the floor.____ Oh, when that

Additional lyrics

3. Baby, I know you're asking me to stay,
   Sayin' please, please, please, don't go way.
   You say I'm giving you the blues,
   Maybe you mean every word you say.
   Can't help but think of yesterday,
   And another who tied me down to loverboy rules.

4. Before this river becomes an ocean,
   Before you throw my heart back on the floor.
   Oh, baby, I reconsider my foolish notion,
   Well, I need someone to hold me,
   But I'll wait for something more.

The First Cut Is The Deepest

Words and Music by
Cat Stevens

Additional lyrics

2., 3. I still want you by my side,
Just to help me dry the tears that I've cried,
And I'm sure gonna give you a try.
If you want, I'll try to love again.
But baby, I'll try to love again but I know.

Folsom Prison Blues

Words and Music by
John R. Cash

Strumming style ↓ ↓ ↑ ↑ ↓ ↓ ↑ ↓ ↓ ↑ ↓ ↓ ↑

1 & a 2 & a 3 & a 4 & a

Moderately

Verse

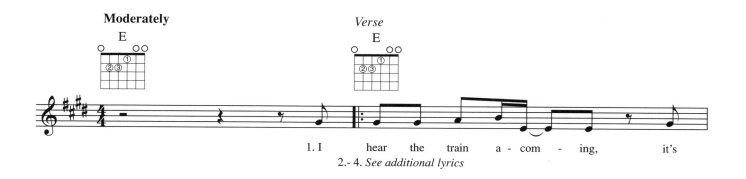

1. I hear the train a-com - ing, it's
2.- 4. *See additional lyrics*

roll - ing round the bend___ and I ain't seen the sun - shine since

I don't___ know when.___ I'm stuck in Fol - som Pri - son

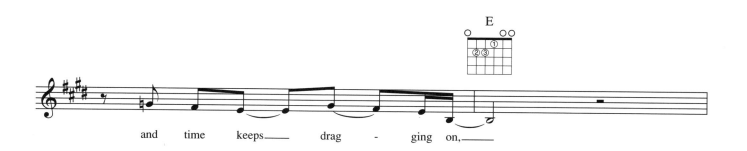

and time keeps___ drag - ging on,___

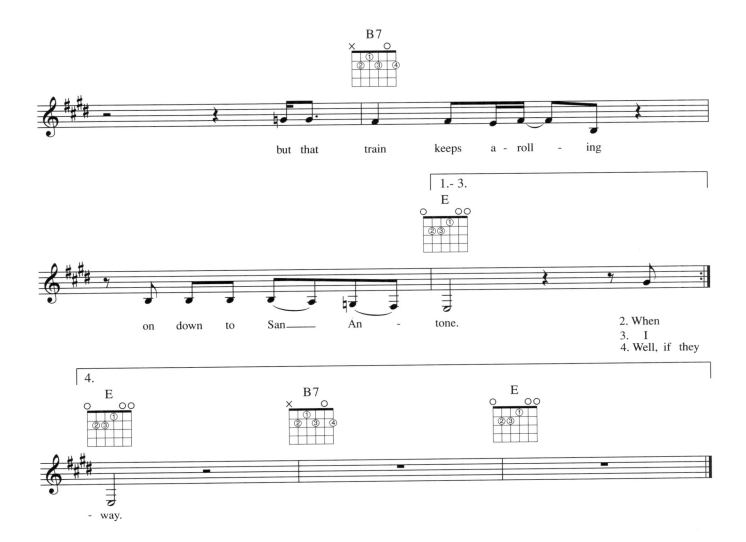

but that   train   keeps   a - roll - ing

on   down   to   San____ An - tone.

2. When
3. I
4. Well, if they

- way.

Additional lyrics

2. When I was just a baby,
   My Mama told me, "Son,
   Always be a good boy,
   Don't ever play with guns."
   But I shot a man in Reno
   Just to watch him die.
   When I hear that whistle blowin',
   I hang my head and cry.

3. I bet there's rich folks eating,
   In a fancy dining car.
   They're probably drinking coffee
   And smoking big cigars.
   Well, I know I had it coming,
   I know I can't be free,
   But those people keep a-movin',
   And that's what tortures me.

4. Well, if they freed me from this prison,
   If that railroad train was mine,
   I bed I'd move out over
   A little farther down the line,
   Far from Folsom Prison,
   That's where I want to stay.
   And I'd let that lonesome whistle,
   Blow my blues away.

Friends In Low Places

Words and Music by
DeWayne Blackwell and Earl Bud Lee

beer chas - es my blues a - way, and I'm

real - ly o - kay. I'm not big on

so - cial grac - es, think I'll slip on down to the

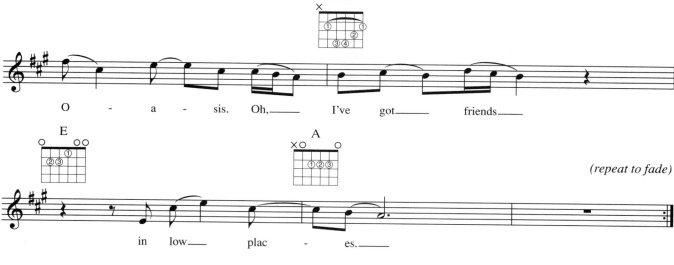

O - a - sis. Oh, I've got friends

(repeat to fade)

in low plac - es.

Additional lyrics

2. I guess I was wrong, I just don't belong,
But then I've been there before.
Everything's alright, I'll just say goodnight,
And I'll show myself to the door.
Hey, I didn't mean to cause a big scene,
Just give me an hour and then,
Well, I'll be as high as that Ivory Tower
But you'll never know...

Father And Son

Words and Music by
Cat Stevens

that it's not ea - sy to be calm when you found some - thing go - ing on. But take your time, think a lot, think of eve - ry thing you've got, for you will still be here to - mor - row but your dreams may not. How can I try to ex - plain? 'Cos when I do he turns a - way a - gain. It's al - ways been the same, same old sto - ry. From the mo - ment I could talk I was or - dered to lis - ten, now there's a way

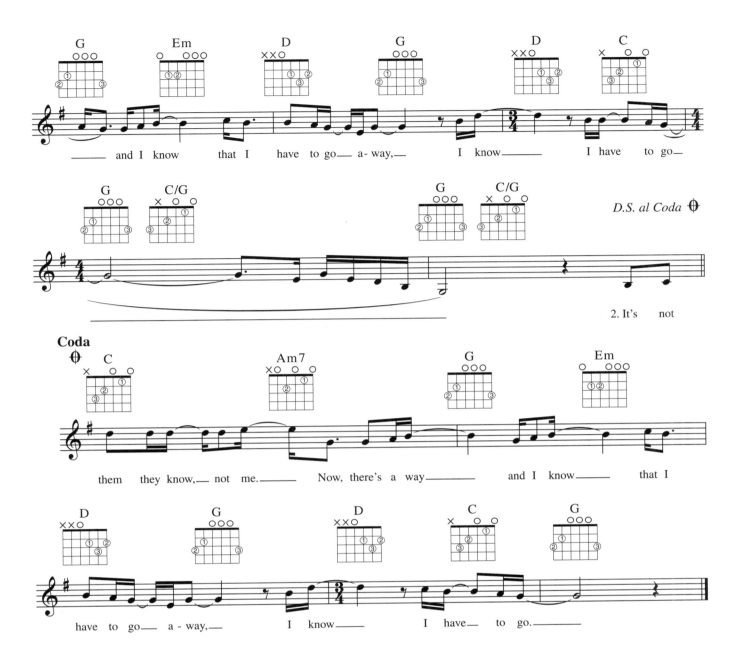

Additional lyrics

2. It's not time to make a change,
   Just sit down, take it slowly.
   You're still young, that's your fault,
   There's so much you have to go through.
   Find a girl, settle down,
   If you want you can marry.
   Look at me, I am old, but I'm happy.

   All the times that I cried,
   Keeping all the things I knew inside,
   It's hard, but it's harder to ignore it.
   If they were right, I'd agree,
   But it's them they know not me.
   Now there's a way and I know that I have to go away.

The Game Of Love

Words and Music by
Rick Nowels and Gregg Alexander

(repeat to fade)

Additional lyrics

2. Love is whatever you make it to be,
   Sunshine instead of this cold lonely sea.
   So please baby,
   Try and use me for what I'm good for.
   It ain't saying goodbye,
   It's knocking down the door of your candy store.

3. So please tell me why
   Don't you come around no more?
   'Cos right now I'm dyin'
   Outside the door
   Of your lovin' store.

Glad All Over

Words and Music by
Dave Clark and Mike Smith

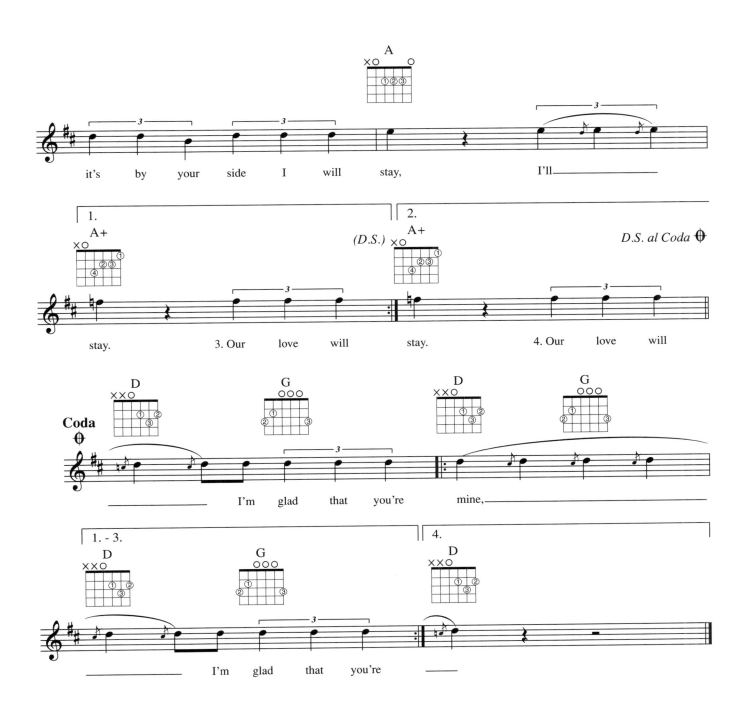

it's   by   your   side   I   will   stay,   I'll_____

1.
stay.   3. Our   love   will   stay.   (D.S.)   4. Our   love   will   *D.S. al Coda*

2.

Coda   I'm   glad   that   you're   mine,_____

1. - 3.   I'm   glad   that   you're   _____   4.

Additional lyrics

2.   I'll make you happy,
     You'll never be blue,
     You'll have no sorrow,
     'Cos I'll always be true.

3., 4. Our love will last now,
     'Til the end of time,
     Because this love now,
     Is gonna be yours and mine.

Get Up, Stand Up

Words and Music by
Bob Marley and Peter Tosh

*Optional capo 2nd fret

that glit-ters is gold,___ half___ the sto - ry has___ nev - er been told.___ So

1. - 2.

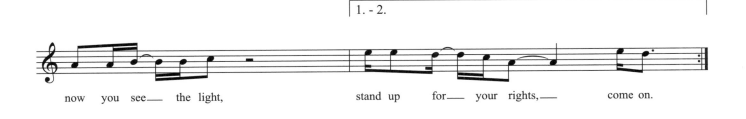

now you see___ the light, stand up for___ your rights,___ come on.

3.

D.C. al Coda ⊕

Coda
⊕

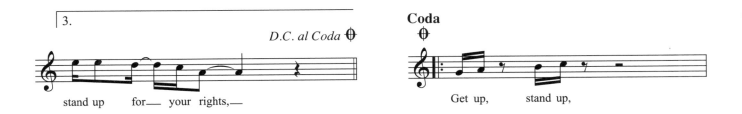

stand up for___ your rights,___   Get up, stand up,

stand up for___ your rights. Get up, stand up, don't give up___ the fight.

Additional lyrics

2. Most people think, Great God will come from the skies,
   Take away everything, and make everybody feel high.
   But if you know what life is worth,
   You will look for yours on earth.
   And now you see the light,
   You stand up for your rights, Jah!

3. We're sick an tired of your "ism-skism" game,
   Dying and going to Heaven in Jesus' name, Lord.
   We know when we understand,
   Almighty God is a living man.
   You can fool some people sometimes,
   But you can't fool all the people all the time.
   So now we see the light, we gonna stand up for our rights.

Gimme Some Lovin'

Words and Music by
Steve Winwood, Muff Winwood and Spencer Davis

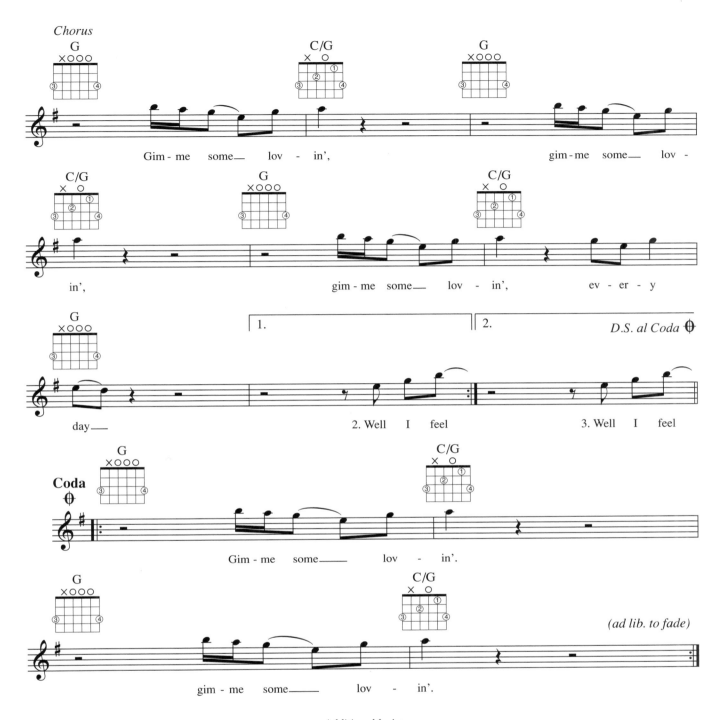

Additional lyrics

2. Well, I feel so good,
   Everything is gettin' higher.
   You better take it easy 'cos the place is on fire.
   Been a hard day and I had some work to do.
   We made it, baby, and it had to be you.
   And I'm so glad we made it,
   So glad we made it.
   You got to...
   Chorus

3. Well, I feel so good,
   Everything is gettin' higher.
   You better take it easy 'cos the place is on fire.
   Been a hard day and nothing went too good.
   Now I'm gonna relax, like everybody should.
   Well, I'm so glad we made it,
   So glad we made it.
   You got to...
   Chorus

Good Girls Don't

Words and Music by
Douglas Fieger

Chorus

Bridge

(play 3 times)

Additional lyrics

2. So, you call her on the phone
   To talk about the teachers that you hate,
   And she says she's all alone,
   And her parents won't be coming home 'til late.
   There's a ringing in your brain,
   'Cos you could've swore you though you heard her saying...
   (Chorus)

3. You're alone with her at last,
   And you're waiting 'til you think the time is right,
   'Cos you've heard she's pretty fast,
   And you're hoping that she'll give you some tonight.
   So you start to make your play,
   'Cos you could've swore you thought you heard her saying...
   (Chorus)

Hallelujah

Words and Music by
Leonard Cohen

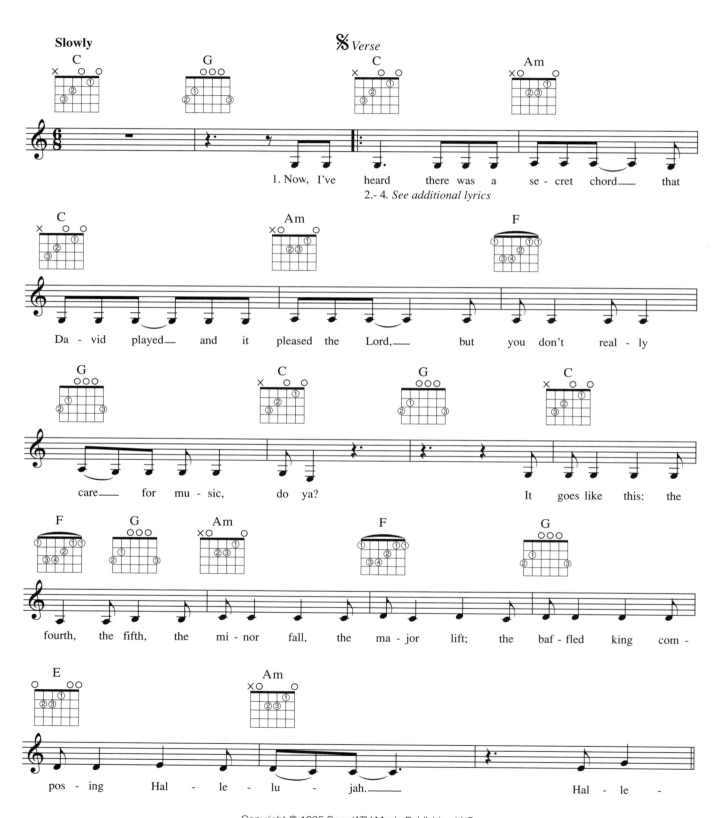

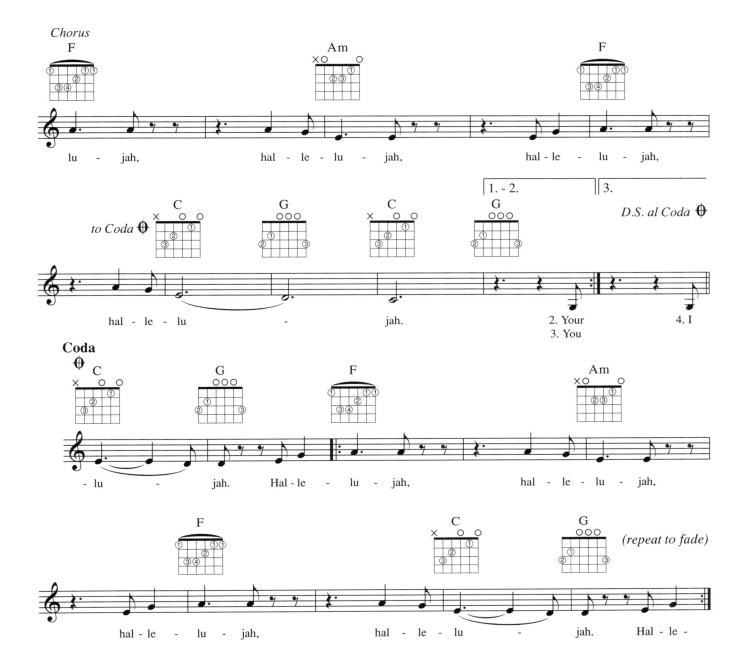

Additional lyrics

2. Your faith was strong but you needed proof,
   You saw her bathing on the roof,
   Her beauty and the moonlight overthrew ya.
   She tied you to a kitchen chair,
   She broke your throne, and she cut your hair,
   And from your lips she drew the Hallelujah.

3. You say I took the name in vain,
   I don't even know the name,
   But if I did, well really, what's it to ya?
   There's a blaze of light in every word,
   It doesn't matter which you heard,
   The holy or the broken Hallelujah.

4. I did my best, it wasn't much,
   I couldn't feel, so I tried to touch;
   I've told the truth, I didn't come to fool ya.
   And even though it all went wrong,
   I'll stand before the Lord of Song
   With nothing on my tongue but Hallelujah.

Hey Joe

Words and Music by
Billy Roberts

Additional lyrics

2. Hey Joe, I heard you shot your woman down,
   You shot her down now,
   Hey Joe, I heard you shot you old lady down,
   You shot her down to the ground, yeah!
   Yes, I did, I shot her,
   You know I caught her messin' 'round,
   Messin' 'round town.
   Yes I did, I shot her,
   You know I caught my old messin' 'round town,
   And I gave her the gun and I shot her!

3. Hey Joe, where you gonna run to now?
   Where you gonna run to?
   Hey Joe, I said where you gonna run to now?
   Where you, where you gonna go?
   Well, dig, I'm goin' way down south,
   Way down to Mexico way, alright!
   I'm goin' way down south,
   Way down where I can be free,
   Ain't no one gonna find me.

Highway To Hell

Words and Music by
Angus Young, Malcolm Young and Bon Scott

Verse
Strumming style (1) (2) (3) & 4 &   ↑ ↓ ↑

Chorus
Strumming style 1 2 3 4 & (1) 2 & 3 4   ↓ ↓ ↓ ↓ ↑ ↓ ↑ ↓ ↓

Moderate Rock

Verse

A   D/F#   G   D/F#   G

1. Liv - in' ea - sy,   liv - in' free,___
2. *See additional lyrics*

D/F#   G   D/F#   A

sea - son tick - et on a   one way___ ride.___

D/F#   G   D/F#   G

Ask - ing noth - ing,   leave___ me be,

D/F#   G   D/F#   A

tak - ing eve - ry - thing___ in my   stride.___

D/F#   G   D/F#   G

Don't___ need rea - son,   don't___ need rhyme,

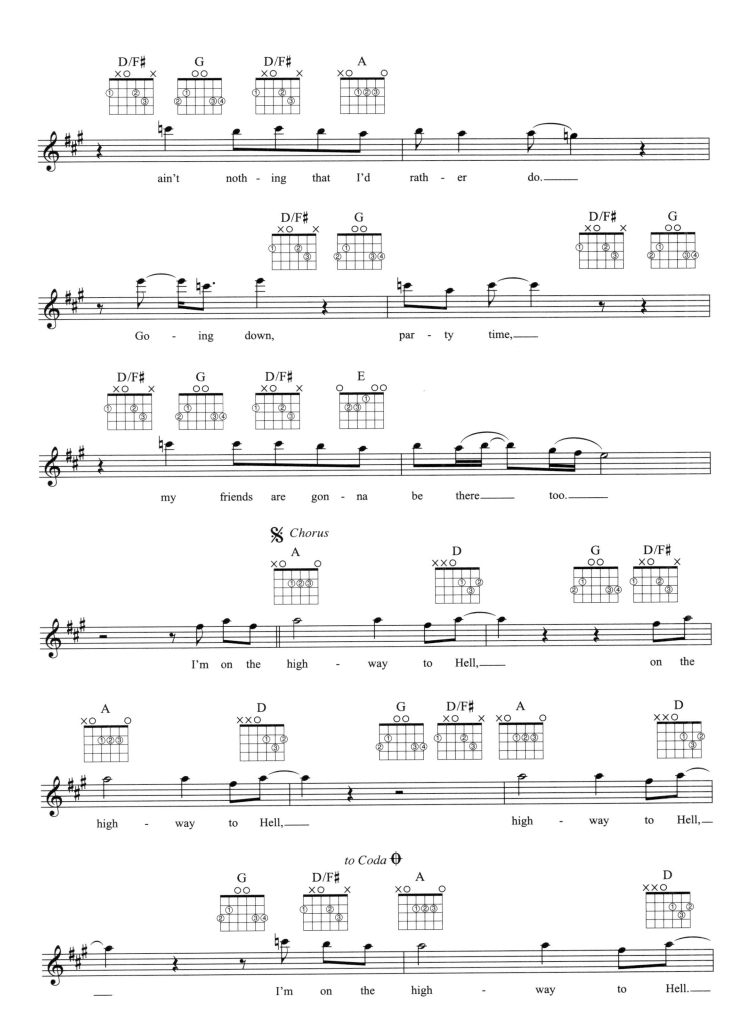

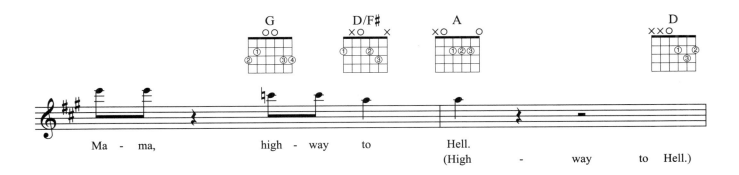

Ma - ma, high - way to Hell.
(High - way to Hell.)

Freely

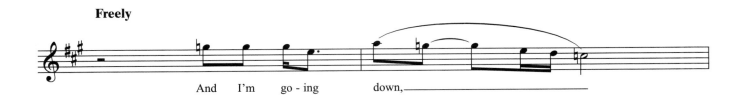

And I'm go - ing down,

all the way. Wow!

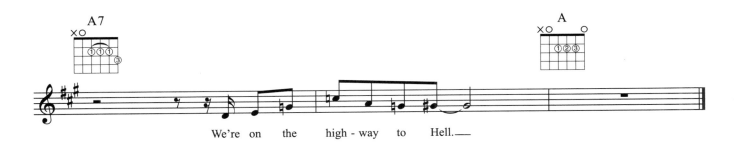

We're on the high - way to Hell.

Additional lyrics

2. No stop signs, speed limit.
Nobody's gonna slow me down.
Like a wheel, gonna spin it,
Nobody's gonna mess me around.
Hey Satan! Paid my dues,
Playin' in a rockin' band.
Hey Mama, look at me,
I'm on my way to the promised land.

Home Sweet Home

Words and Music by
Nikki Sixx, Vince Neil and Tommy Lee

Additional lyrics

2. You know that I've seen
   Too many romantic dreams
   Up in lights, falling off the silver screen.
   My heart's like an open book
   For the whole world to read;
   Sometimes nothing keeps me together at the seams.

Honky Tonk Women

Words and Music by
Mick Jagger and Keith Richards

Additional lyrics

2. I layed a divorcée in New York City,
   I had to put up some kind of a fight,
   The lady, then she covered me with roses,
   She blew my nose and then she blew my mind.

He Ain't Heavy, He's My Brother

Words and Music by
Bob Russell and Robert William Scott

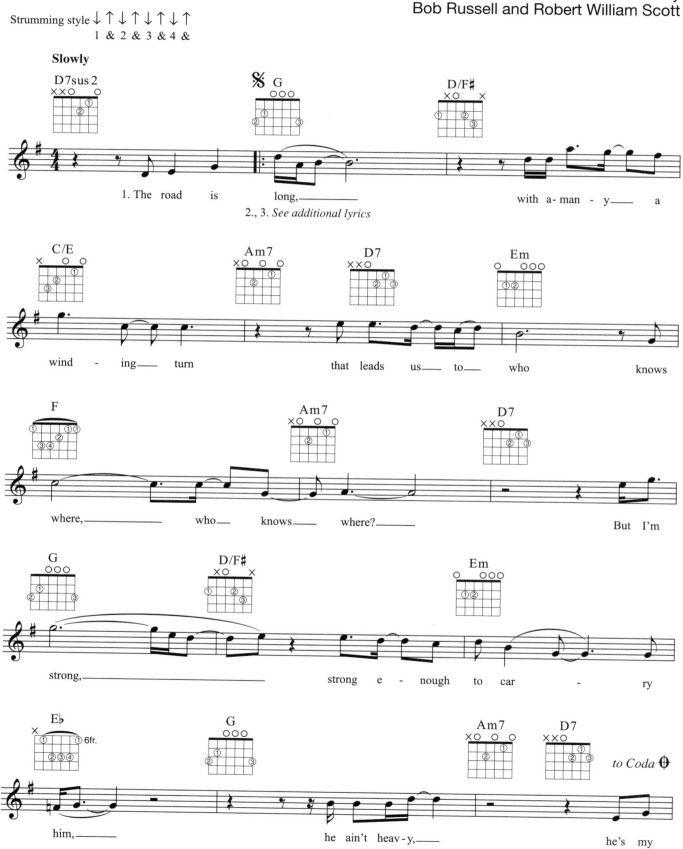

Coda

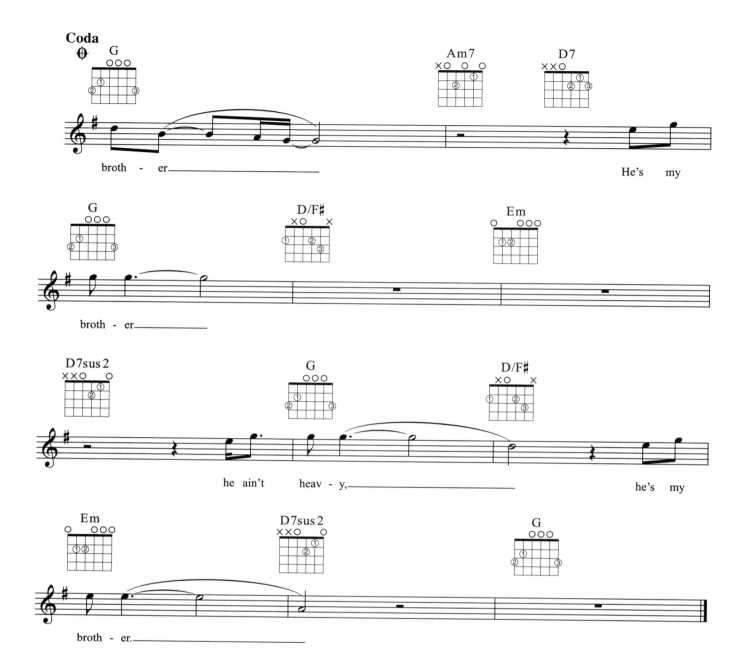

broth - er_____ He's my

broth - er_____

he ain't heav - y,_____ he's my

broth - er._____

Additional lyrics

2. So on we go,
   His welfare is of my concern,
   No burden is he to bear.
   We'll get there,
   For I know he would not encumber me.
   He ain't heavy, he's my brother.

3. It's a long, long road,
   From which there is no return.
   While we're on the way to there,
   Why not share?
   And the load doesn't weigh me down at all.
   He ain't heavy, he's my brother.

If It Makes You Happy

Words and Music by
Sheryl Crow and Jeff Trott

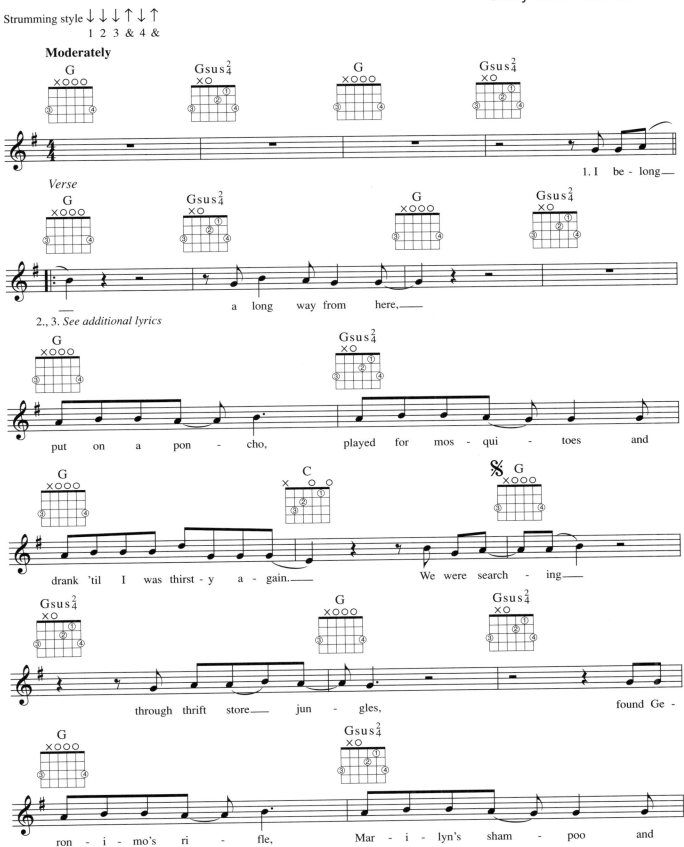

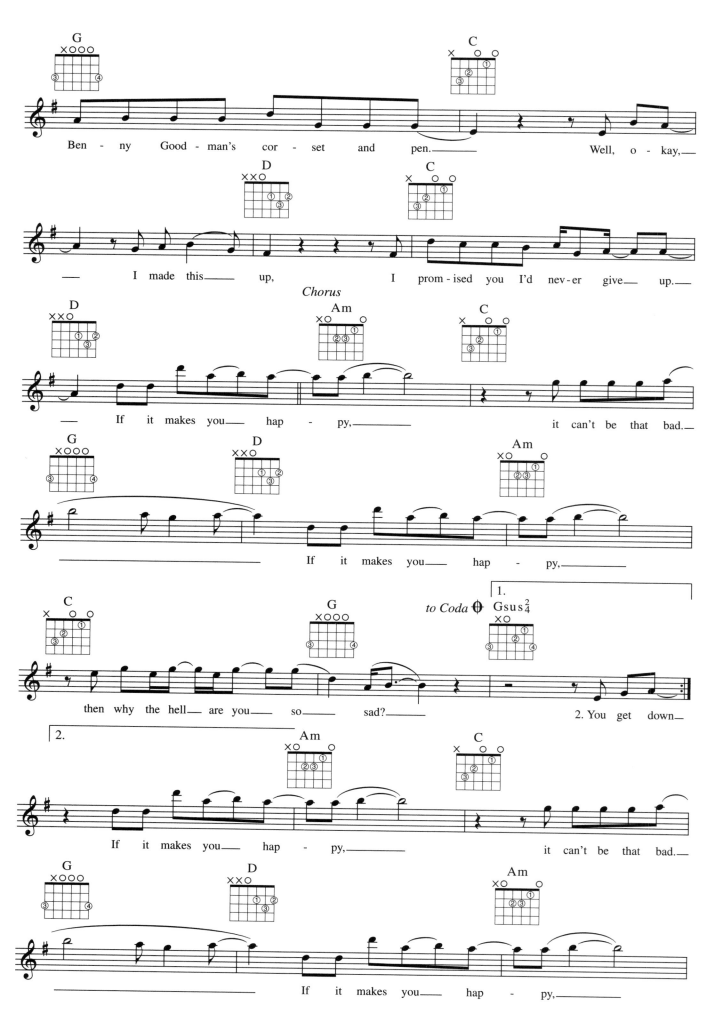

Ben - ny Good - man's cor - set and pen._____ Well, o - kay,___

— I made this____ up, I prom - ised you I'd nev - er give__ up.___

Chorus

— If it makes you___ hap - py,_____ it can't be that bad.___

If it makes you___ hap - py,_____

then why the hell__ are you__ so___ sad?_____

2. You get down___

If it makes you___ hap - py,_____ it can't be that bad.___

If it makes you___ hap - py,_____

126

then why the hell are you so sad?

D.S. al Coda

3. We've been far,

Coda

If it makes you hap - py, it can't be that bad.

If it makes you hap - py,

then why the hell are you so sad?

Additional lyrics

2. You get down, real low down,
   You listen to Coltrane, derail your own train,
   Well, who hasn't been there before?
   I come round, around the hard way,
   Bring you comics in bed, scrape the mold off the bread,
   And serve you French toast again,
   Well, okay, I still get stoned.
   I'm not the kind of girl you'd take home.

3. We've been far, far away from here,
   Put on a poncho, played for mosquitoes,
   And everywhere in between.
   Well, okay, we get along,
   So what if right now everything's wrong?

I Walk The Line

Words and Music by
John R. Cash

self _____ a - lone _____ when each day's through. Yes, I'll ad -

mit that I'm a fool for you, be - cause you're

mine, I walk the line.

Mm. _____ 3. As sure as

night is dark and day is light, I keep you

on my mind both day and night. And hap - pi -

ness   I've   known   proves———   that   it's   right,

be - cause   you're

mine,   I   walk   the   line.

Mm._____

4. You've   got   a

way   to   keep   me   on——   your——   side,

you   give   me

cause   for   love   that   I____   can't____   hide.

For   you   I

know   I'd   e - ven   try   to   turn   the   tide,

be - cause   you're

mine,   I   walk   the   line.

Mm.———————————————— 5. I keep a

close   watch   on   this   heart   of   mine,   I   keep   my

eyes   wide   o - pen   all   the   time.   I   keep   the

ends   out   for   the   tie——   that   binds,——   be - cause——   you're

(repeat to fade)

mine,   I   walk   the   line.

I'm A King Bee

Words and Music by
James H. Moore

Strumming style ↓ ↑ ↓ ↑ ↓ ↑ ↓ ↑
1 & 2 & 3 & 4 &

Moderate swing

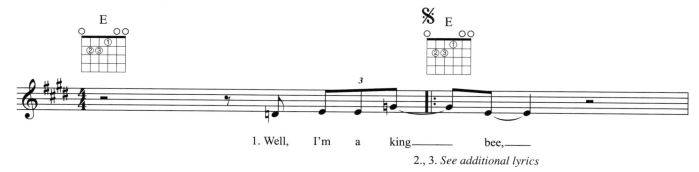

1. Well, I'm a king_____ bee,_____

2., 3. *See additional lyrics*

buzz - ing a - round_____ your hive._____

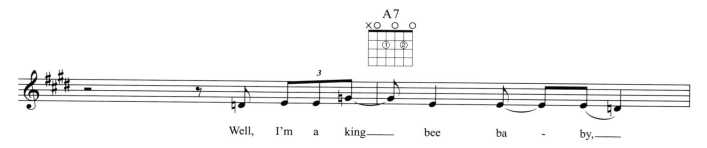

Well, I'm a king_____ bee ba - by,_____

buzz - ing a - round_____ your hive._____

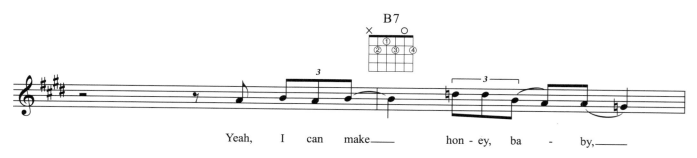

Yeah, I can make_____ hon - ey, ba - by,_____

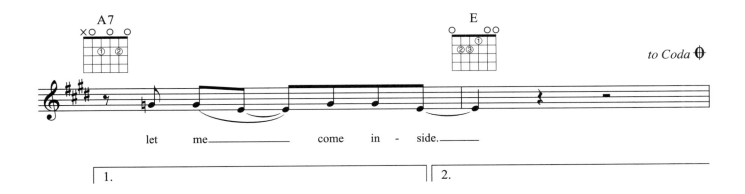

to Coda ⊕

let me   come in - side.

1.   2.

2. Well, I'm a king   Well,

D.S. al Coda ⊕

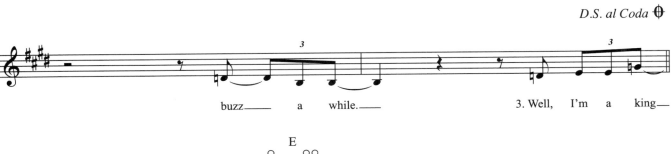

buzz   a while.   3. Well, I'm a king

Coda
⊕

E

(repeat to fade)

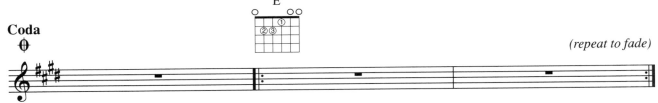

Additional lyrics

2. Well, I'm a king bee,
   Want you to be my queen.
   Well I'm a king bee, baby,
   Want you to be my queen.
   Together we can make honey
   The world has never seen.

3. Well I'm a king bee,
   Can buzz all night long.
   Well I'm a king bee, baby,
   Can buzz all night long.
   Yeah I can buzz better, baby,
   When your man is gone.

In The Midnight Hour

Words by Wilson Pickett
Music by Steve Cropper

Strumming style ↓ ↓ ↑ ↓ ↓ ↑

1 2 & 3 4 &

Moderately

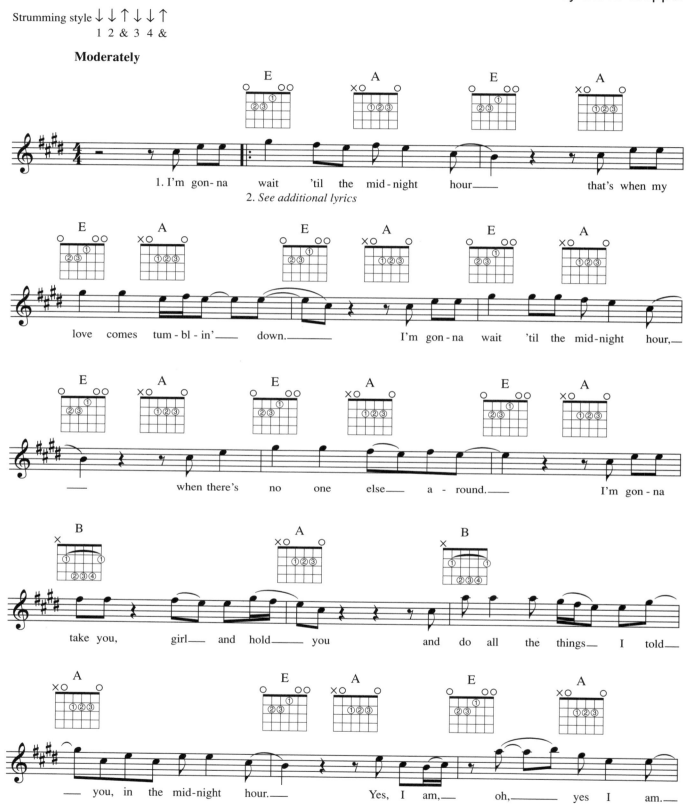

1. I'm gon-na wait 'til the mid-night hour____ that's when my

2. *See additional lyrics*

love comes tum-bl-in'____ down.____ I'm gon-na wait 'til the mid-night hour,____

____ when there's no one else____ a-round.____ I'm gon-na

take you, girl____ and hold____ you and do all the things____ I told____

____ you, in the mid-night hour.____ Yes, I am,____ oh,____ yes I am.____

Additional lyrics

2. I'm gonna wait 'til the stars come out,
   And see that twinkle in your eyes.
   I'm gonna wait 'til the midnight hour,
   That's when my love begins to shine.
   You're the only girl I know,
   That can really love me so,
   In the midnight hour.

Iris

Words and Music by
John Rzeznik

me, 'cos I don't___ think that they'd___ un - der -

stand. When eve - ry - thing's made to be bro -

- ken, I just want___ you to know___ who I am.

1.

D.S.

3. And you

2.

D.S.S. al Coda

And I

Coda

And I don't want the world___ to see___

I've Seen All Good People
(Your Move/All Good People)

Words and Music by
Jon Anderson and Chris Squire

Your Move ↓ ↑ ↓ ↑   ↑ ↓ ↑ ↓ ↑ ↑   ↑ ↓ ↑
Strumming style 1 a & a (2) a & a 3 a & a (4) a & a

All Good People ↓   ↑ ↓   ↑ ↓   ↑ ↓   ↑
Strumming style 1 (&) a 2 (&) a 3 (&) a 4 (&) a

Fast

N.C.

I've seen all good peo - ple turn their heads

each day, so sat - is - fied, I'm on

Your Move

Slowly

E   F♯m/E

my way.

G♯m/E   F♯m/E   E   F♯m/E

1. Take a straight and strong - er course to the
2., 3. *See additional lyrics*

G♯m/E   F♯m/E   E   F♯m/E

cor - ner of your life, make the White Queen run so fast,

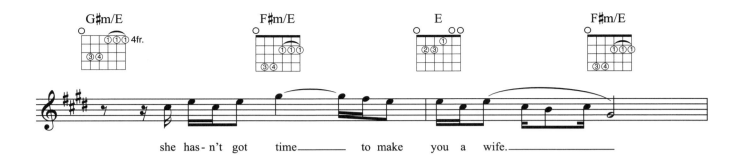

she has-n't got time———— to make you a wife.————

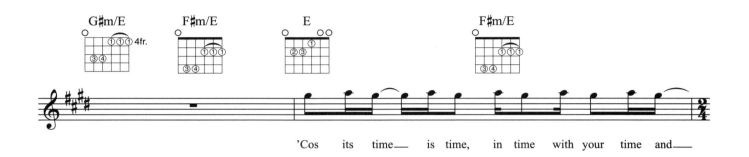

'Cos its time— is time, in time with your time and——

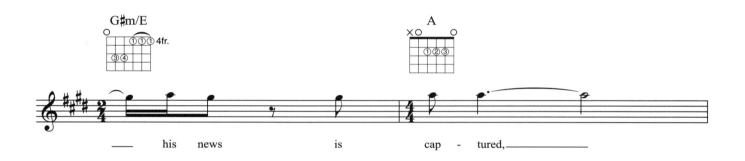

—— his news is cap - tured,————

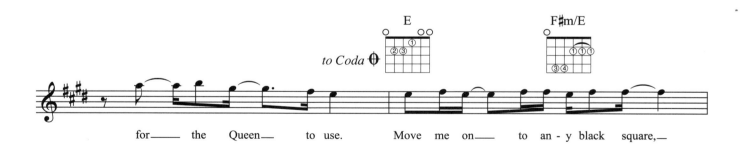

to Coda ⊕

for—— the Queen— to use. Move me on— to an-y black square,—

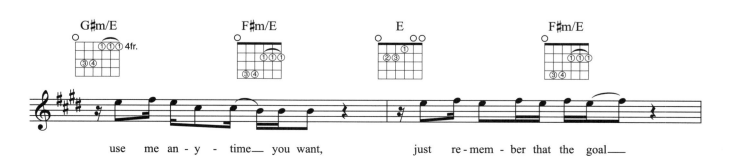

use me an-y - time— you want, just re-mem - ber that the goal——

140

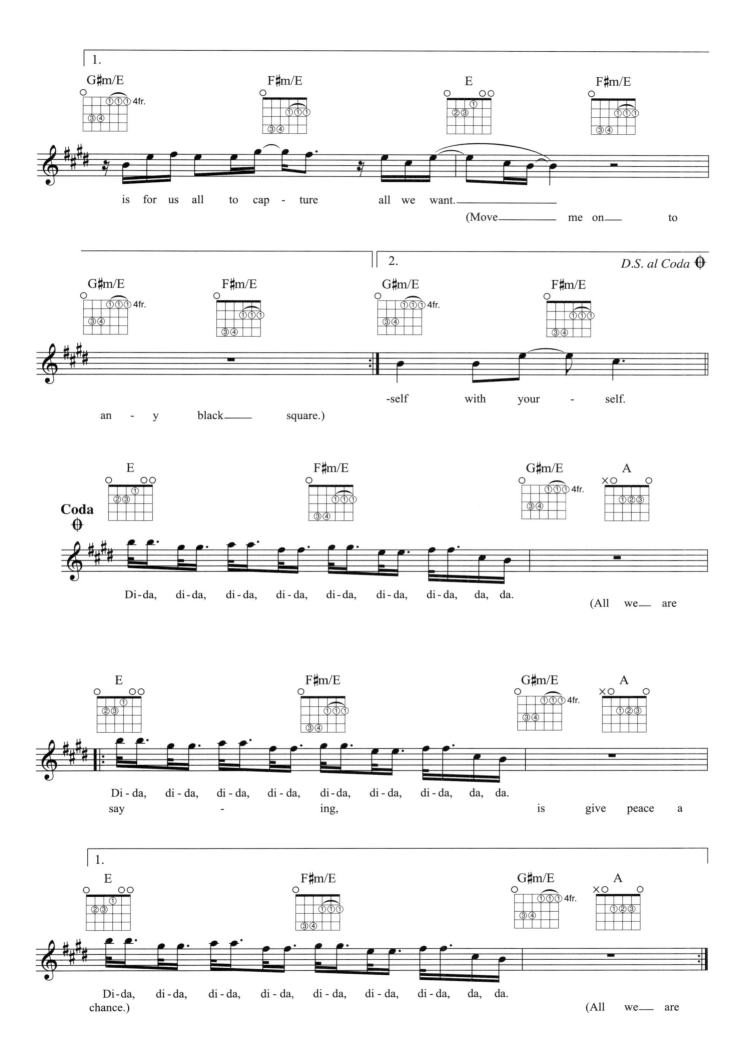

'Cos its time____ is time, in time with your time and____
chance.)

____ its news is cap - tured,____

All Good People

Fast

I've seen all___ good___ peo - ple___ turn___ their___ heads___

___ each___ day,___ so___ sat - is - fied,___ I'm___ on___

___ my___ way.___

Additional lyrics

2., 3. Don't surround yourself with yourself,
Move on back two squares,
Send an instant karma to me,
Initial it with loving care, yourself,

'Cos its time is time, in time,
With your time and its news is captured,
For the queen to use.
Dida, dida, dida, dida,
Dida, dida, dida, da, da.
Don't surround yourself with yourself.

Island In The Sun

Words and Music by
Rivers Cuomo

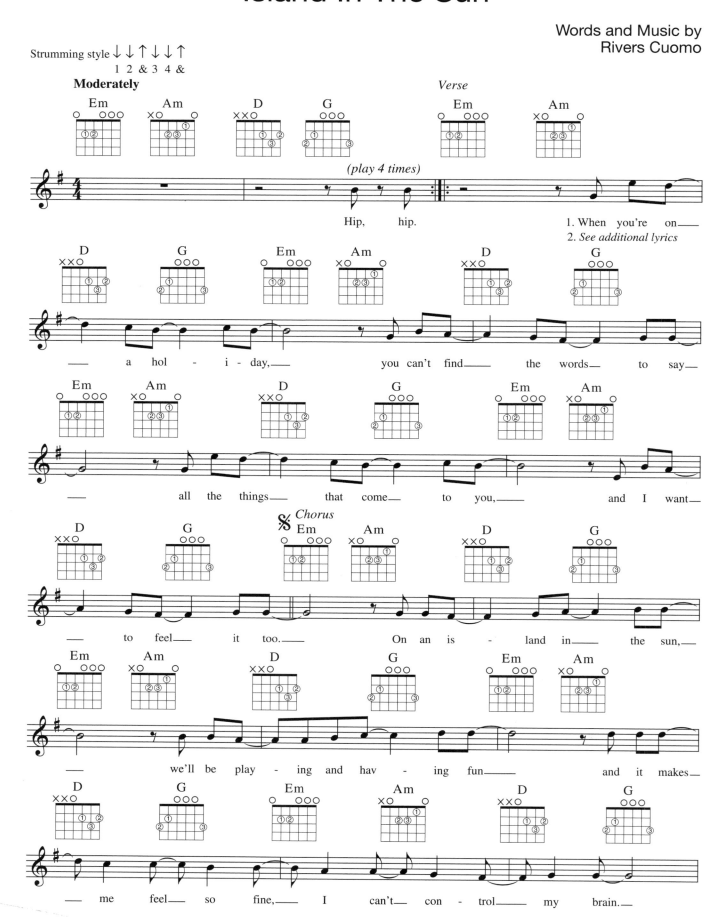

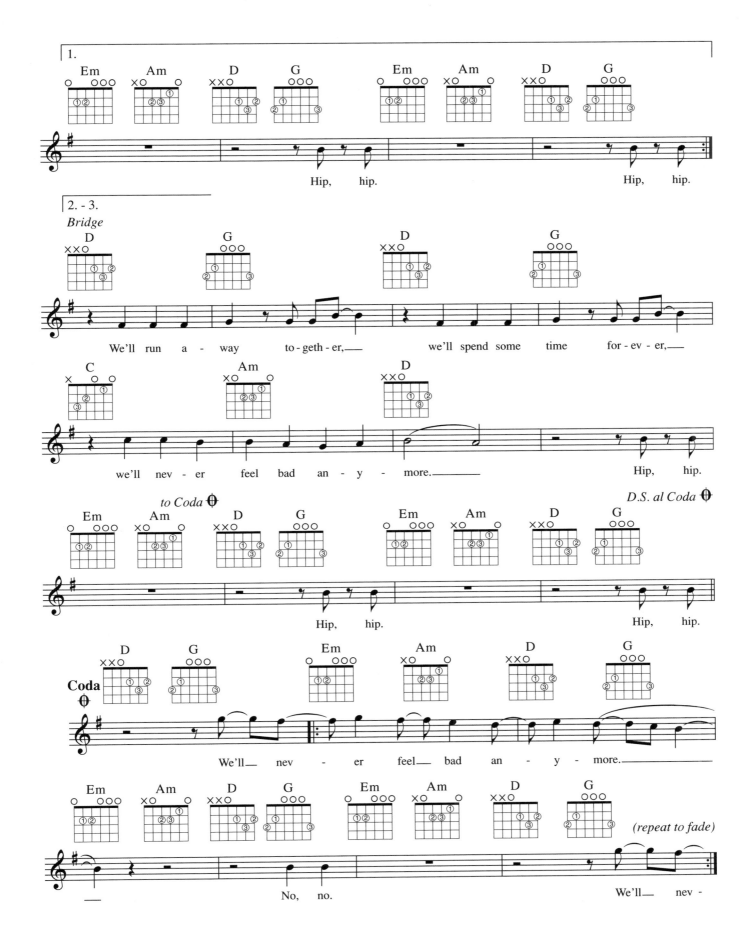

to Coda ✪

D.S. al Coda ✪

Additional lyrics

2. When you're on a golden sea,
   You don't need no memory,
   Just a place to call your own,
   As we drift into the zone.

Just Like Heaven

Words and Music by
Robert Smith, Laurence Tolhurst, Simon Gallup,
Paul S. Thompson and Boris Williams

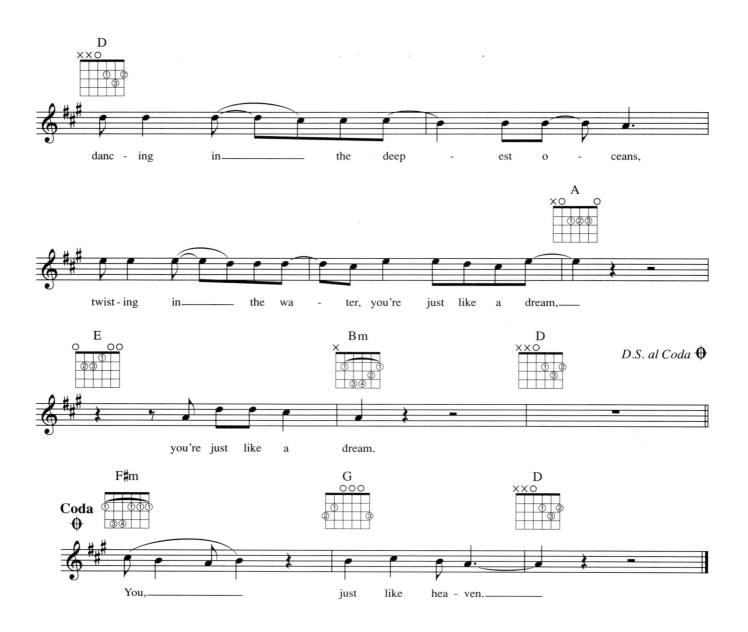

Additional lyrics

2. Spinning on that dizzy edge,
   I kissed her face and kissed her head,
   And dreamed of all the different ways
   I had to make her glow.
   "Why are you so far away?" she said,
   "Why won't you ever know that I'm in love with you,
   That I'm in love with you."

3. Daylight licked me into shape,
   I must have been asleep for days,
   And moving lips to breathe her name,
   I opened up my eyes,
   And found myself alone, alone,
   Alone above a raging sea,
   That stole the only girl I loved,
   And drowned her deep inside of me.

Keep On Loving You

Words and Music by
Kevin Cronin

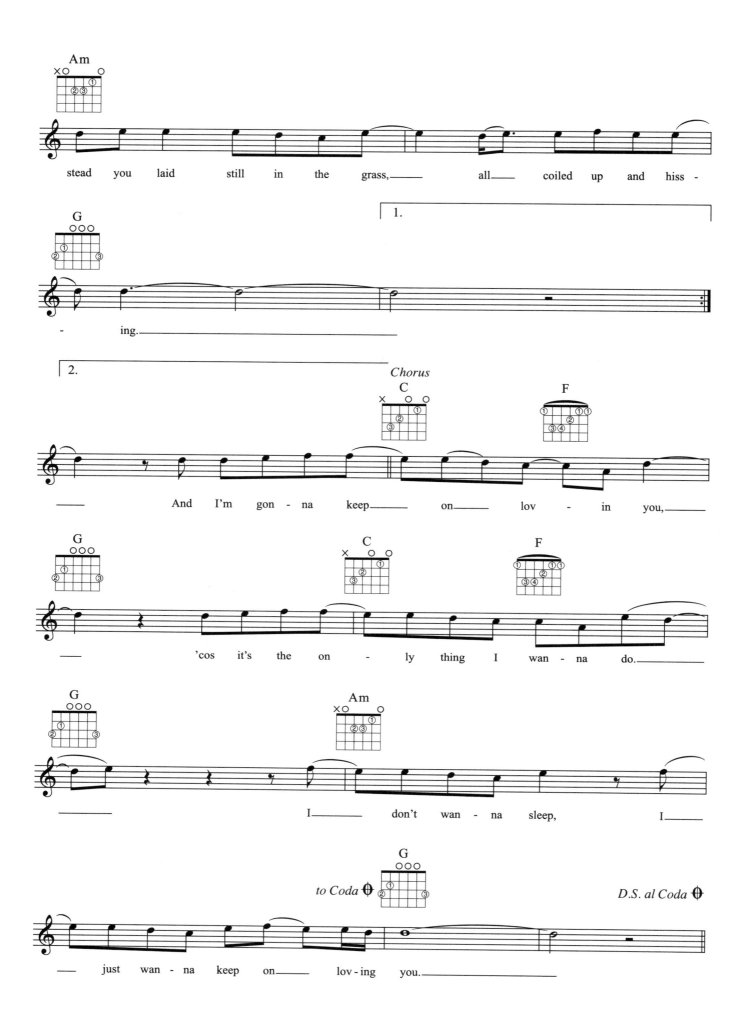

stead you laid still in the grass,_____ all_____ coiled up and hiss -

1.

- ing._____

2. *Chorus*

_____ And I'm gon - na keep_____ on_____ lov - in you,_____

_____ 'cos it's the on - ly thing I wan - na do._____

_____ I_____ don't wan - na sleep, I_____

to Coda ⊕   *D.S. al Coda* ⊕

_____ just wan - na keep on_____ lov - ing you._____

Coda

you._____ Ba - by, I'm gon - na keep____

____ on lov - ing you,_____ 'cos it's the on -

- ly thing I wan - na do._____ I____

____ don't wan - na sleep, I____ just wan - na keep on____ lov - ing

you._____

Additional lyrics

2. And though I know all about those men,
   Still I don't remember.
   'Cos it was us baby, way before them,
   And we're still together.
   And I meant every word I said,
   When I said that I love you,
   I meant that I'd love you forever.

3. And I meant every word I said,
   When I said that I love you,
   I meant that I'd love you forever.

Layla

Words and Music by
Eric Clapton and Jim Gordon

Verse
Strumming style 1

Chorus
Strumming style 1

Moderately

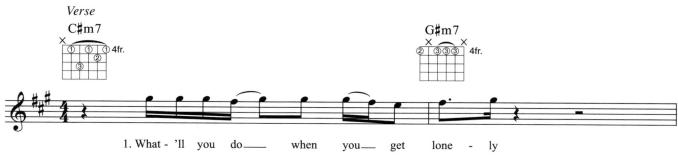

1. What - 'll you do____ when you____ get lone - ly
2., 3. *See additional lyrics*

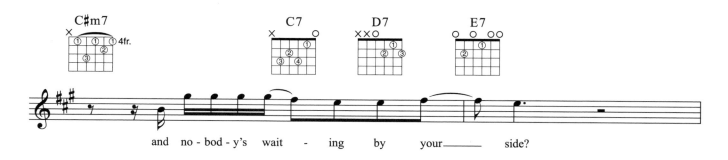

and no - bod - y's wait - ing by your____ side?

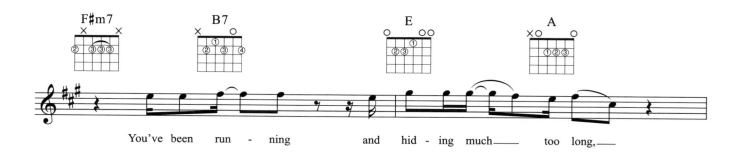

You've been run - ning and hid - ing much____ too long,____

you know, it's just____ your fool - ish pride. Lay -

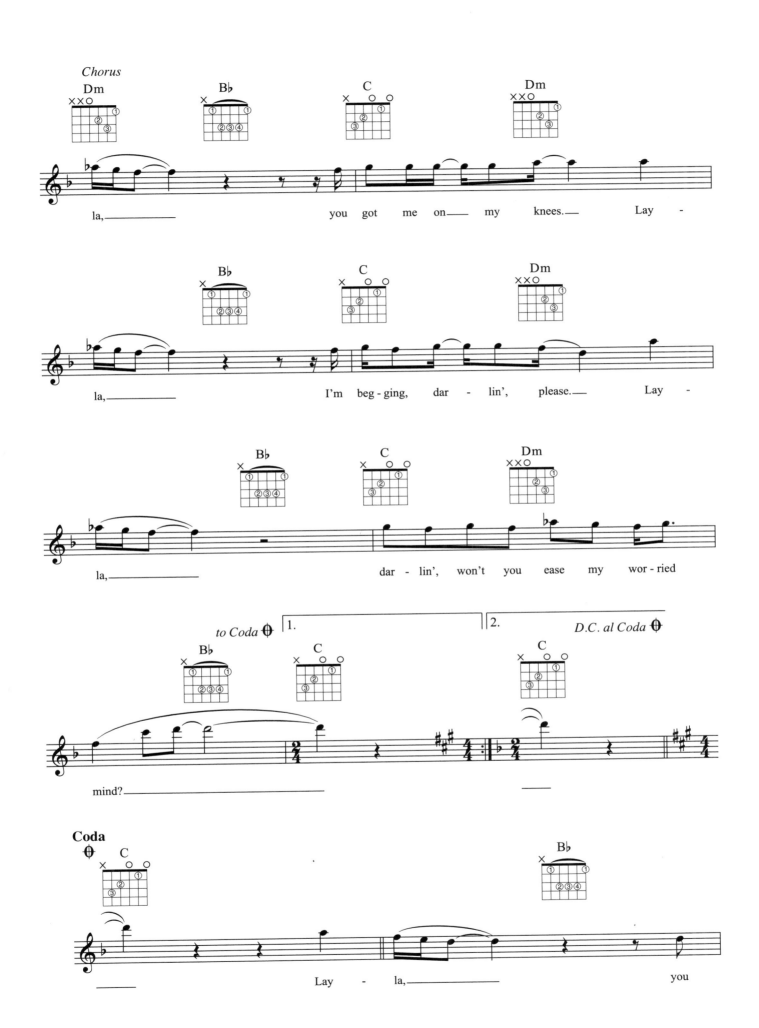

got me on— my knees.— Lay - la,————————— I'm

beg - ging, dar - lin', please.— Lay - la,——————————

dar - lin', won't you ease my wor - ried mind?————————————————

(repeat to fade)

Additional lyrics

2. I tried to give you consolation,
   When your old man had let you down.
   Like a fool, I fell in love with you;
   Turned my whole world upside down.
   (Chorus)

3. Let's make the best of the situation,
   Before I finally go insane.
   Please don't say we'll never find a way,
   And tell me all my love's in vain.
   (Chorus)

Like A Rolling Stone

Words and Music by
Bob Dylan

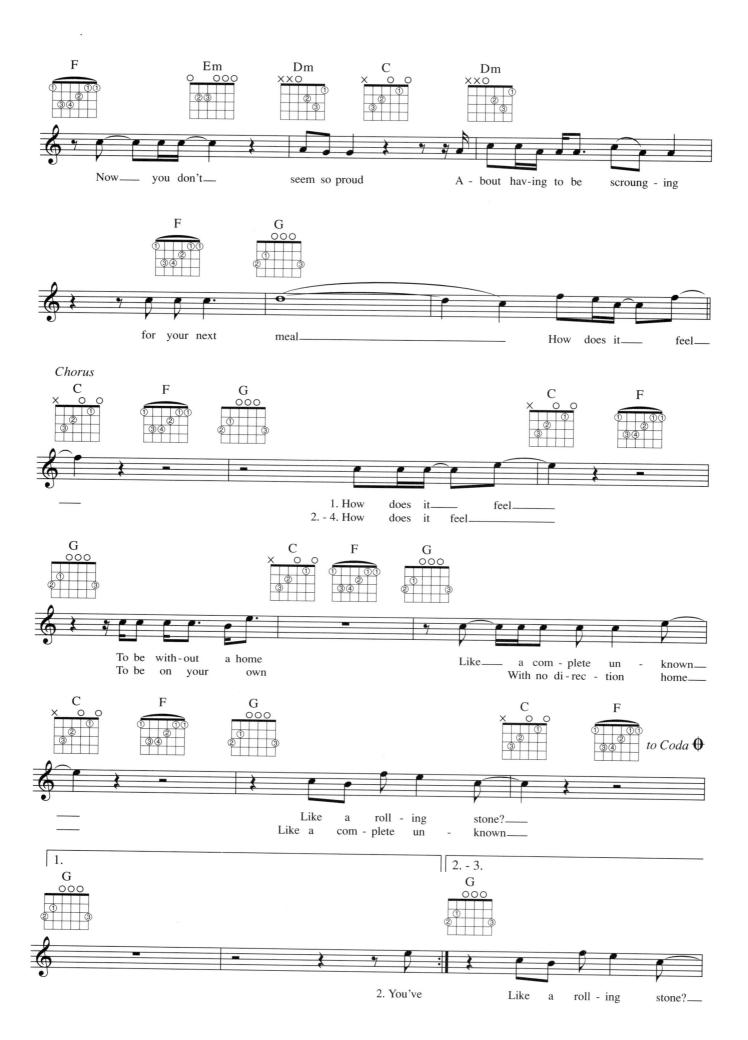

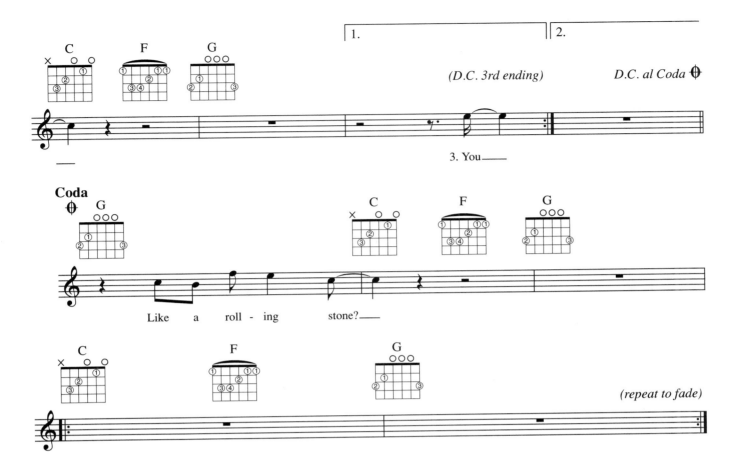

(D.C. 3rd ending)

D.C. al Coda

3. You——

Coda

Like a roll - ing stone?——

(repeat to fade)

Additional lyrics

2. You've gone to the finest school all right, Miss Lonely
   But you know you only used to get juiced in it
   And nobody has ever taught you how to live on the street
   And now you find out you're gonna have to get used to it
   You said you'd never compromise
   With the mystery tramp, but now you realize
   He's not selling any alibis
   As you stare into the vacuum of his eyes
   And ask him do you want to make a deal?
   Chorus

3. You never turned around to see the frowns on the jugglers and the clowns
   When they all come down and did tricks for you
   You never understood that it ain't no good
   You shouldn't let other people get your kicks for you
   You used to ride on the chrome horse with your diplomat
   Who carried on his shoulder a Siamese cat
   Ain't it hard when you discover that
   He really wasn't where it's at
   After he took from you everything he could steal
   Chorus

4. Princess on the steeple and all the pretty people
   They're drinkin', thinkin' that they got it made
   Exchanging all kinds of precious gifts and things
   But you'd better lift your diamond ring, you'd better pawn it babe
   You used to be so amused
   At Napoleon in rags and the language that he used
   Go to him now, he calls you, you can't refuse
   When you got nothing, you got nothing to lose
   You're invisible now, you got no secrets to conceal
   Chorus

Life Is A Highway

Words and Music by
Tom Cochrane

Chorus
Strumming style (1) & (2) a (&) 3   4

Verse
Strumming style 1 & 2 & 3 & 4 &

Moderately

Verse

B♭

1. Love's like a road that you trav-el on, where there's one___
2., 3. *See additional lyrics*

F

___ day here___ and the next___ day gone.___ Some-times___

C

___ you bend,___ some-times___ you stand,___ some-

times you turn___ your back___ to the wind.___ There's a world___

B♭

___ out-side___ the dark-ened door___ where

F

blues won't haunt___ you an-y-more, where the

brave are free__ and lov - ers soar.__ Come ride__ with me__ to the dis - tant shore.__

We won't hes - i - tate,__ break down the gar - den gate,__

there's not much time left to - day.__

Chorus

Life is a high - way, I__ wan - na ride__ it all__

__ night long.__ If

you're go - ing my__ way, I__ wan - na drive__ it all__

1.

__ night long.__

2. Through all__

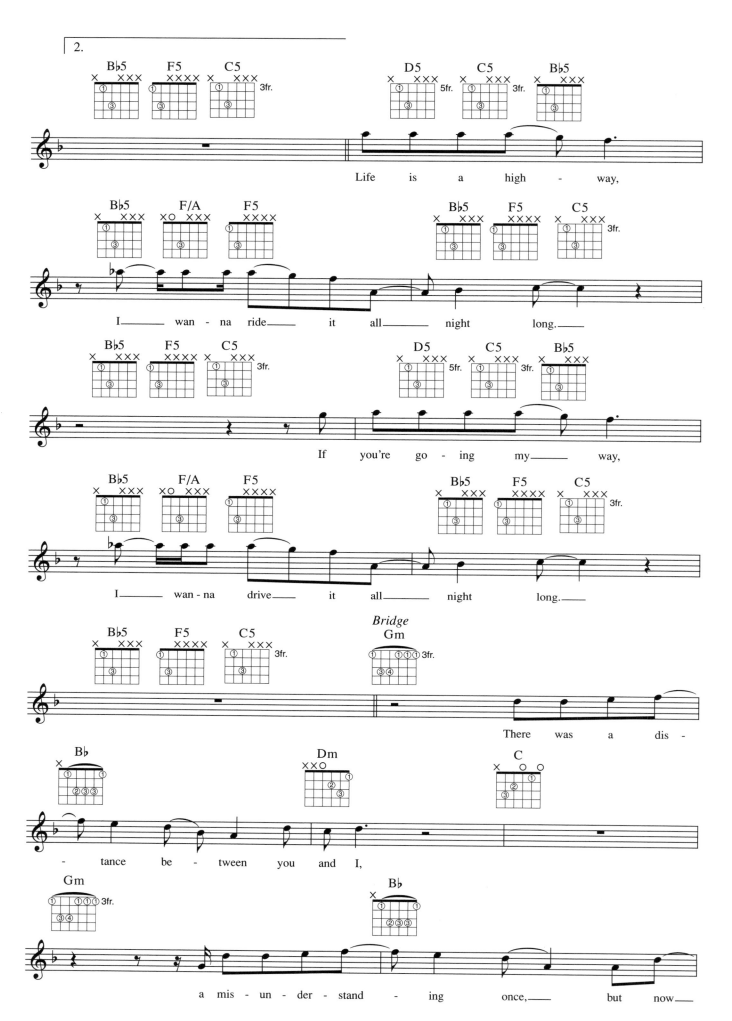

Additional lyrics

2. Through all these cities and all these towns,
   It's in my blood and it's all around.
   I love you now like I loved you then,
   This is the road and these are the hands.
   From Mozambique to those Memphis nights,
   The Khyber Pass to Vancouver's lights,
   Knock me down, get back up again,
   You're in my blood, I'm not a lonely man.
   There's no load I can't hold,
   Road so rough; this I know.
   I'll be there when the light comes in,
   Just tell 'em we're survivors.

3. There ain't no load that I can't hold,
   Road so rough; this I know,
   I'll be there when the light comes in,
   Just tell 'em we're survivors.

Love Hurts

Words and Music by
Boudleaux Bryant

Strumming style ↓ ↓ ↑ ↓ ↓ ↑
1 2 & 3 4 &

Slowly

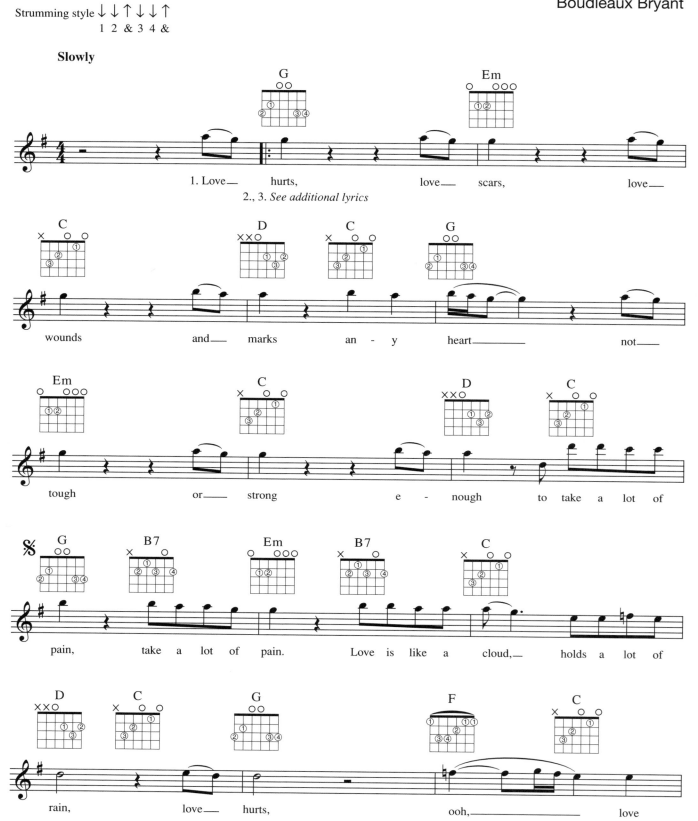

1. Love— hurts, love— scars, love—

2., 3. See additional lyrics

wounds and— marks an - y heart_____ not—

tough or— strong e - nough to take a lot of

pain, take a lot of pain. Love is like a cloud,— holds a lot of

rain, love— hurts, ooh,_____ love

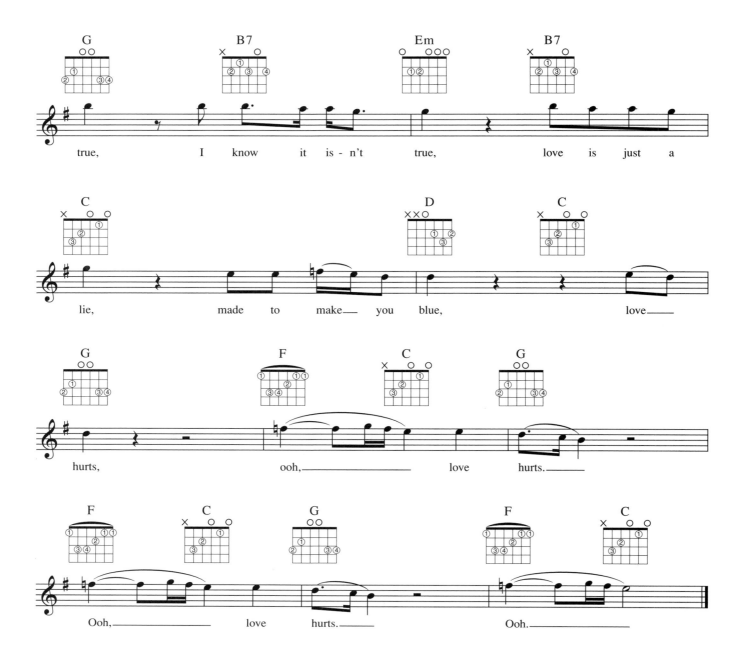

Additional lyrics

2. I'm young, I know,
   But even so,
   I know a thing or two,
   I learned from you,
   I really learned a lot,
   Really learned a lot,
   Love is like a flame,
   It burns you when it's hot.
   Love hurts, ooh, love hurts.

3. I know it isn't true,
   I know it isn't true,
   Love is just a lie,
   Made to make you blue,
   Love hurts, ooh, love hurts.

Mr. Jones

Words by Adam Duritz
Music by Adam Duritz and David Bryson

Strumming style ↓ ↓ ↓ ↑ ↓ ↑
        1 2 3 & 4 &

Moderately

(2nd time only) dance the si - lence down through the morn - ing, tra - la - la - la, la - la, la - la,

Tra - la - la, la - la -

la, la, uh - huh.
— yeah.
Uh - huh, yeah.

Verse

1. I was down at the New Am - ster - dam, star - ing at this yel -
2., 3. *See additional lyrics*

low - haired girl. Mis - ter Jones strikes up a con - ver - sa -

- tion with this black - haired fla - men - co dan - cer. You know, she

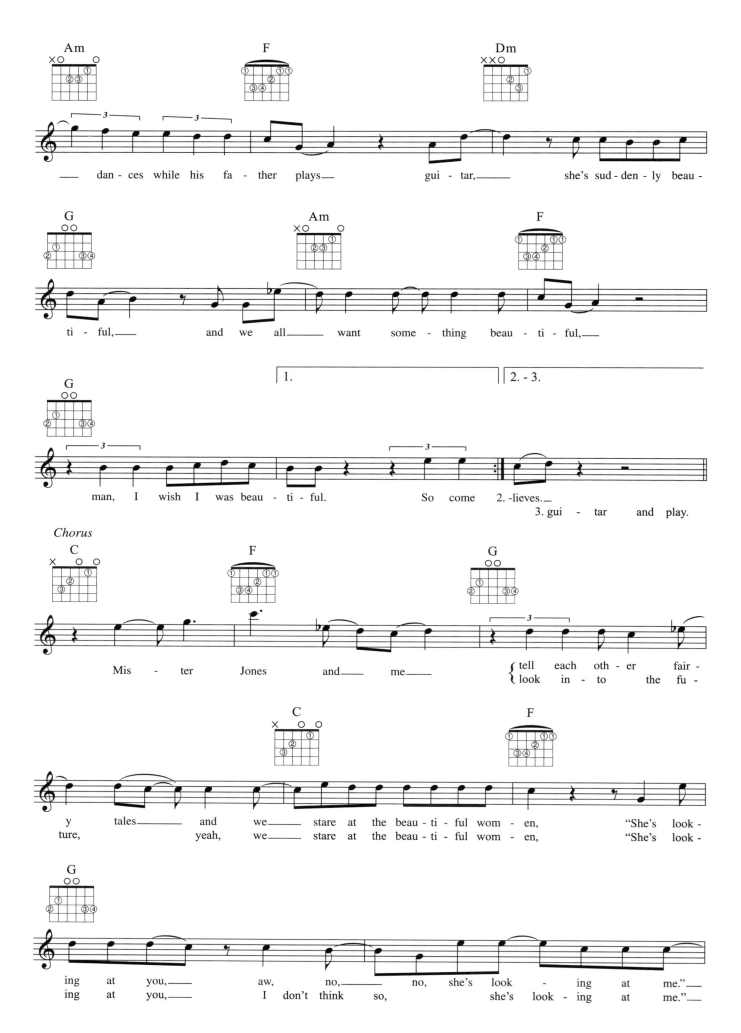

dan - ces while his fa - ther plays___ gui - tar,_____ she's sud - den - ly beau -

ti - ful,___ and we all___ want some - thing beau - ti - ful,___

1.

2. - 3.

man, I wish I was beau - ti - ful. So come 2. -lieves.___

3. gui - tar and play.

Chorus

Mis - ter Jones and___ me___ { tell each oth - er fair -
{ look in - to the fu -

y tales___ and we___ stare at the beau - ti - ful wom - en, "She's look -
ture, yeah, we___ stare at the beau - ti - ful wom - en, "She's look -

ing at you,___ aw, no,___ no, she's look - ing at me."___
ing at you,___ I don't think so, she's look - ing at me."___

C   F   G

  ___ Smil - ing in the bright___ lights,   com - ing through in ster -
  ___ Stand - ing in the spot - light,   I bought my - self a gray___

C   F

- e - o,___ when eve - ry - bod - y love_____ you,
 ___ gui - tar,___ when eve - ry - bod - y love_____ me,

G

to Coda ⊕   *D.S. al Coda* ⊕

you can nev - er be lone - ly.___ 3. Well I'm___
I will nev - er be lone -

Bridge
Am

Coda
⊕

- - ly.___   I will nev - er be lone -
(See additional lyrics)

Fmaj7   Am

- ly, said I'm___ nev - er gon - na be___

1. - 2.   3.

G

lone - ly.___   - be - lieve, yeah.___

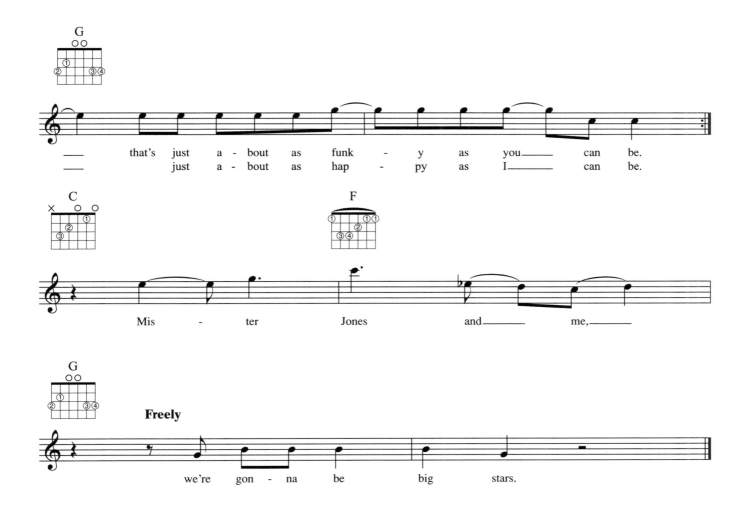

that's just a - bout as funk - y as you_____ can be.
just a - bout as hap - py as I_____ can be.

Mis - ter Jones and_____ me,_____

Freely

we're gon - na be big stars.

Additional lyrics

2. Cut up Maria,
   Show me some of them Spanish dances,
   And pass me a bottle, Mr. Jones.
   Believe in me, help me believe in anything,
   'Cos I wanna be someone who believes.

3. Well, I'm gonna paint my picture,
   Paint myself in blue and red and black and gray,
   All of the beautiful colors are very, very meaningful.
   Yeah, well you know gray is my favorite color;
   I felt so symbolic yesterday,
   If I knew Picasso, I would buy myself a gray guitar and play.

Bridge:
   I want to be a lion,
   Everybody wants to pass as cats,
   We all want to be big, big stars,
   Yeah, but we got different reasons for that,
   Believe in me 'cos I don't believe in anything,
   And I want to be someone to believe,
   To believe, to believe, yeah.

Mammas Don't Let Your Babies Grow Up To Be Cowboys

Words and Music by
Ed Bruce and Patsy Bruce

he'll prob - 'bly just ride— a - way.

Chorus

Mam - mas,— don't let your ba - bies grow up to be cow - boys.—

Don't let 'em pick gui - tars and drive them old trucks,

let 'em be doc - tors and law - yers and such.

Mam - mas,— don't let your ba - bies grow up to be cow - boys,—

'cos they'll nev - er stay home and they're al - ways a - lone,—

e - ven with some - one they love.——

Verse

E

2. Cow - boys like smok - y old pool - rooms and clear moun - tain morn -

A　　　**B**

\- ings, lit - tle warm pup - pies and

E

child - ren and girls of the night._____

Them that don't know him won't like him and them that do

A

some - times won't know how to take_____ him. He ain't

B

wrong, he's just dif - fer - ent but his pride won't let him_____ do

E

things to make you think he's right.

Me And Julio Down By The Schoolyard

Words and Music by
Paul Simon

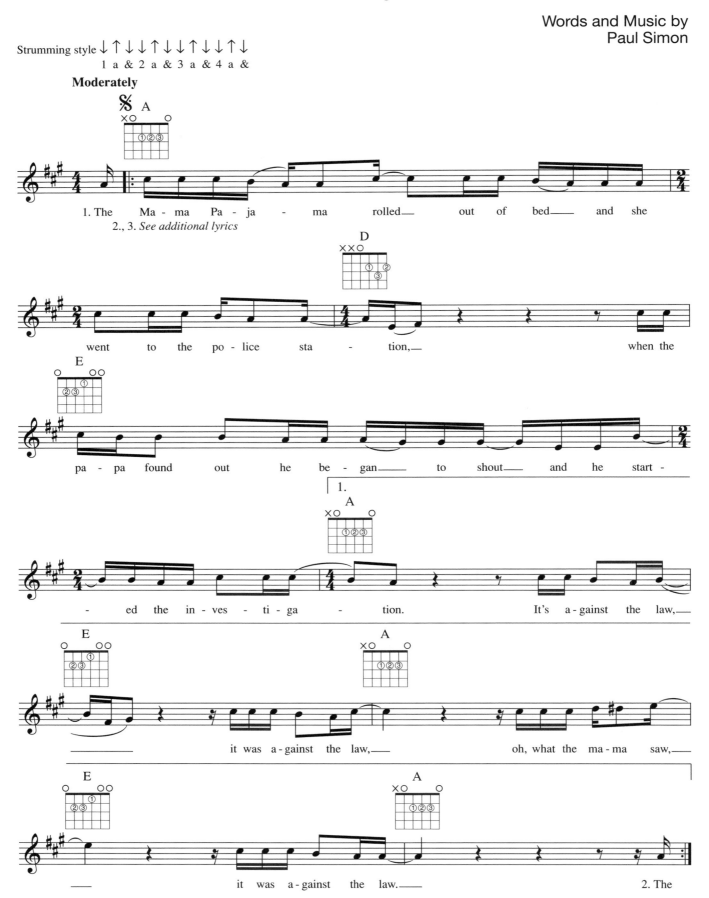

Additional lyrics

2. The mama looked down and spit on the ground,
   Everytime my name gets mentioned,
   The papa said, "Oy if I get that boy,
   I'm gonna stick him in the house of detention."

3. In a couple of days they come and take me away,
   But the press let the story leak,
   And when the radical priest,
   Come to get me released,
   We was all on the cover of *Newsweek*.

Melissa

Words and Music by
Gregg Allman and Steve Alaimo

Additional lyrics

2. Freight train, each car looks the same,
And no one knows the gypsy's name,
No one hears his lonely sigh,
There are no blankets where he lies,
In all his deepest dreams the gypsy flies,
With sweet Melissa.

3. Crossroads, will you ever let him go?
Will you hide the dead man's ghost,
Or will he lie, beneath the clay,
Or will his spirit roll away?
But I know that he won't stay,
Without Melissa.

More Than A Feeling

Words and Music by
Tom Scholz

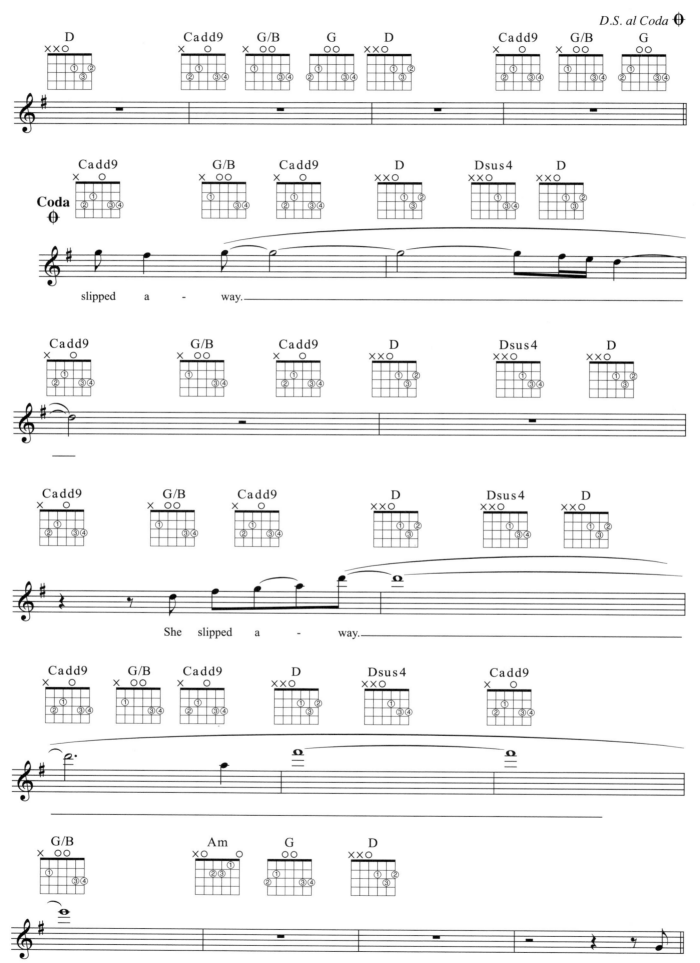

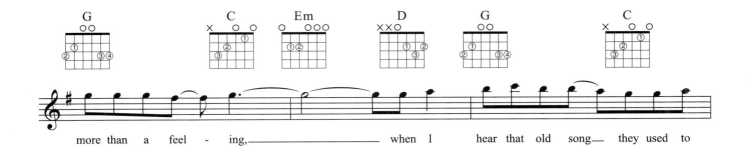

more than a feel - ing,_____ when I hear that old song— they used to

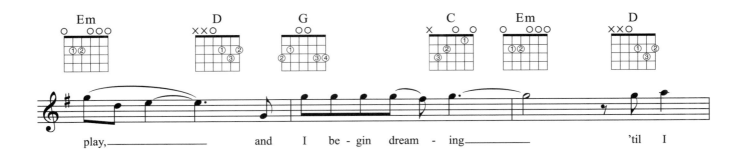

play,_____ and I be - gin dream - ing_____ 'til I

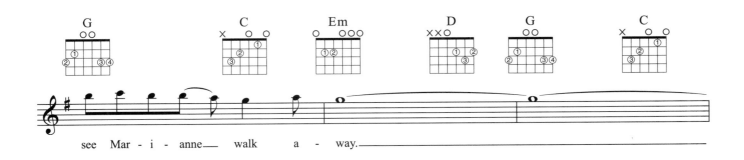

see Mar - i - anne— walk a - way._____

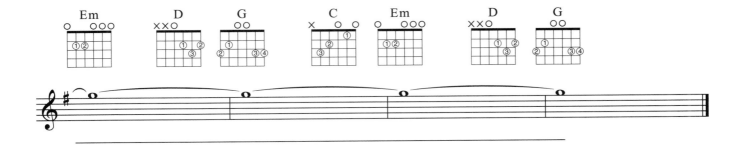

Additional lyrics

2. So many people have come and gone;
   Their faces fade as the years go by.
   Yet I still recall as I wander on,
   As clear as the sun in the summer sky.

3. When I'm tired and thinking cold,
   I hide in my music, forget the day.
   And dream of a girl I used to know;
   I closed my eyes and she slipped away,
   She slipped away, she slipped away.

Mr. Tambourine Man

Words and Music by
Bob Dylan

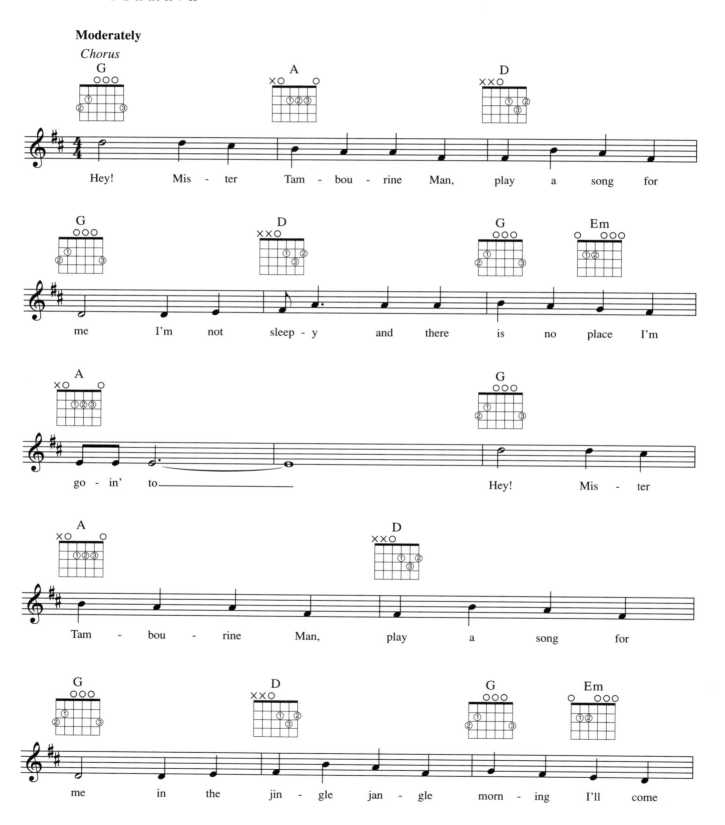

Strumming style ↓ ↓ ↑ ↑ ↓ ↑
1 2 & (3) & 4 &

Moderately

Chorus

Hey! Mis - ter Tam - bou - rine Man, play a song for

me I'm not sleep - y and there is no place I'm

go - in' to____ Hey! Mis - ter

Tam - bou - rine Man, play a song for

me in the jin - gle jan - gle morn - ing I'll come

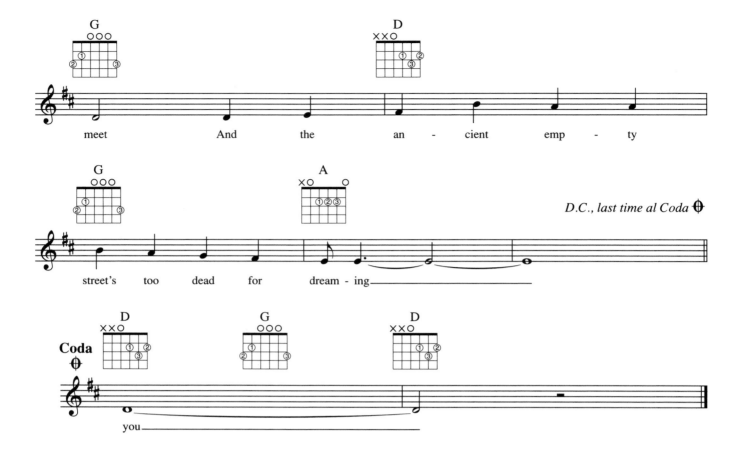

D.C., last time al Coda ⊕

meet   And   the   an - cient   emp - ty

street's   too   dead   for   dream - ing_____

Coda
⊕

you_____

Additional lyrics

2. Take me on a trip upon your magic swirlin' ship
   My senses have been stripped, my hands can't feel to grip
   My toes too numb to step
   Wait only for my boot heels to be wanderin'
   I'm ready to go anywhere, I'm ready for to fade
   Into my own parade, cast your dancing spell my way
   I promise to go under it
   (Chorus)

3. Though you might hear laughin', spinnin', swingin' madly across the sun
   It's not aimed at anyone, it's just escapin' on the run
   And but for the sky there are no fences facin'
   And if you hear vague traces of skippin' reels of rhyme
   To your tambourine in time, it's just a ragged clown behind
   I wouldn't pay it any mind
   It's just a shadow you're seein' that he's chasin'
   (Chorus)

4. Then take me disappearin' through the smoke rings of my mind
   Down the foggy ruins of time, far past the frozen leaves
   The haunted, frightened trees, out to the windy beach
   Far from the twisted reach of crazy sorrow
   Yes, to dance beneath the diamond sky with one hand waving free
   Silhouetted by the sea, circled by the circus sands
   With all memory and fate driven deep beneath the waves
   Let me forget about today until tomorrow
   (Chorus)

My Best Friend's Girl

Words and Music by
Ric Ocasek

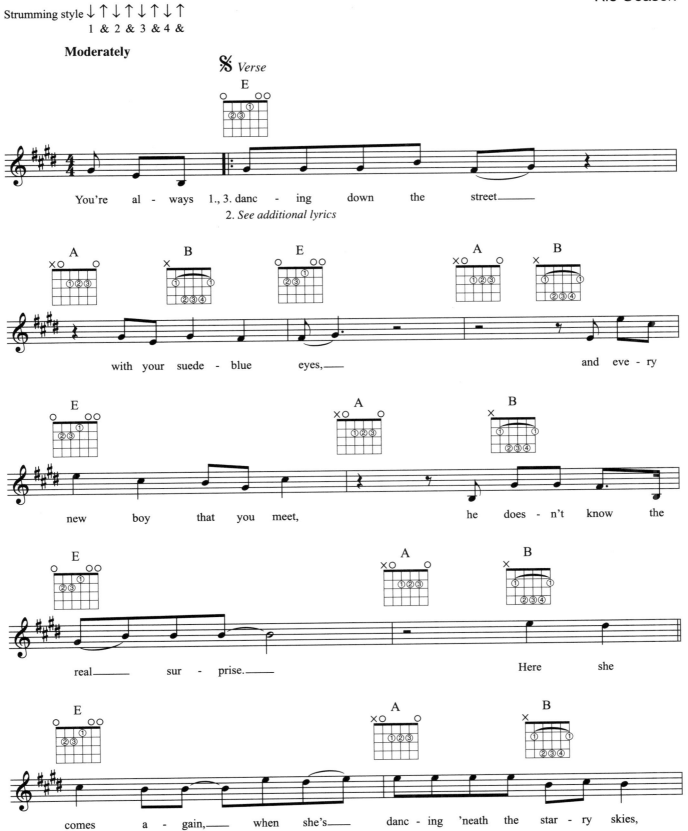

ooh,___ she'll make you flinch. (Here she

comes a - gain.)___ When she's___ danc - ing 'neath the star - ry skies,___

___ I kin - da like the way she dips.

Chorus

'Cos she's my best friend's

girl, She's my best friend's

girl,___ but she used to be mine.___

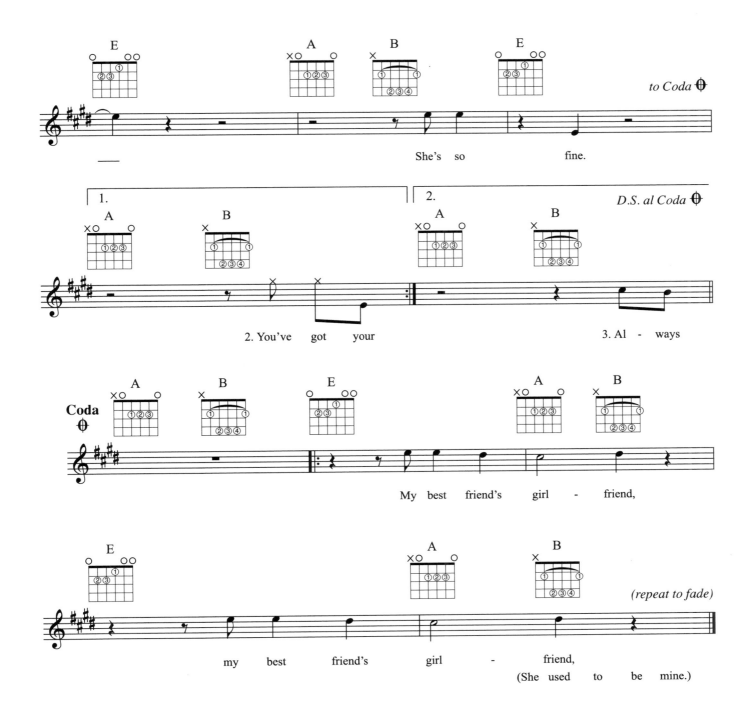

to Coda

She's so   fine.

1.

2.   *D.S. al Coda*

2. You've   got   your

3. Al - ways

Coda

My   best   friend's   girl - friend,

(repeat to fade)

my   best   friend's   girl - friend,

(She used   to   be   mine.)

Additional lyrics

2. You've got your nuclear boots,
And your drip-dry glove.
Ooh, when you bite your lip,
It's some reaction to love.
Here she comes again,
When she's dancing 'neath the starry sky,
Yeah, I think you'll flip.
Here she comes again,
When she's dancing 'neath the starry sky,
Here she comes again,
I kinda like the way, I like the way she dips.

Peace Train

Words and Music by
Cat Stevens

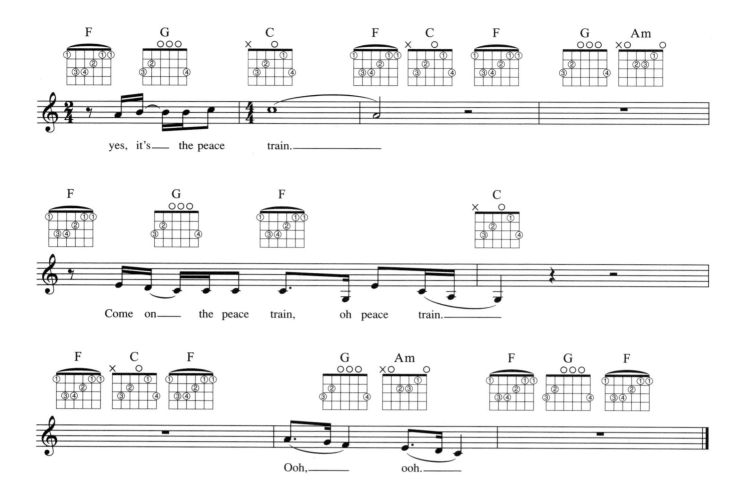

yes, it's — the peace train. —

Come on — the peace train, oh peace train. —

Ooh, — ooh. —

Additional lyrics

2. 'Cos out on the edge of darkness,
   There rides a peace train.
   Oh, peace train take this country,
   Come take me home again.
   Now, I've been smiling lately,
   Thinking about the good things to come,
   And I believe it could be,
   Something good has begun.

3. Get your bags together,
   Go bring your good friends too,
   'Cos it's getting nearer,
   It soon will be with you.
   Now come and join the living,
   It's not so far from you,
   And it's getting nearer,
   Soon it will all be true.

4. Now I've been crying lately,
   Thinking about the world as it is.
   Why must we go on hating,
   Why can't we live in bliss?
   'Cos out on the edge of darkness,
   There rides a peace train.
   Oh, peace train take this country,
   Come take me home again.

No Woman, No Cry

Words and Music by
Vincent Ford

Strumming style ↓ ↓ ↑ ↓ ↓ ↑
1 2 & 3 4 &

Moderately

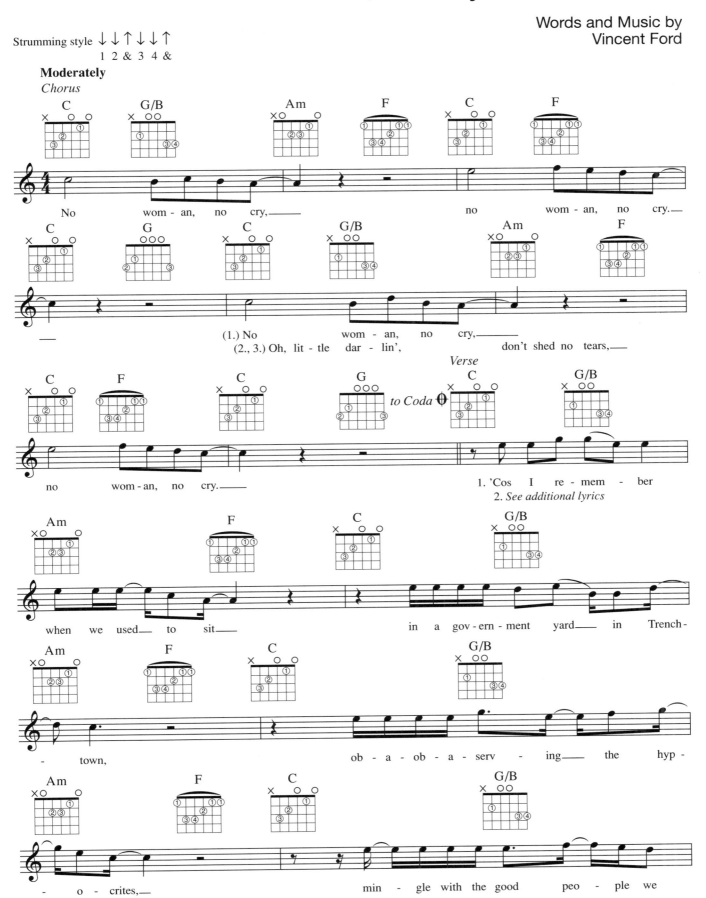

meet.   Good   friends   we   have,   oh,

good   friends— we have lost,   a - long   the   way.——

In   this   great   fu - ture,—   you   can't   for - get   your past,—

1.

so—   dry your tears,—   I   say.

2.   *Bridge*

But   while   I'm   gone,   Eve - ry - thing's gon - na be   al - right,

eve - ry - thing's gon - na be   al - right,   eve - ry - thing's gon - na be   al - right,—

D.C. al Coda

Coda

Additional lyrics

2. I remember when-a we used to sit,
   In the government yard in Trenchtown,
   And then Georgie would make the fire lights,
   I say, a log-a-wood burning through the nights.
   Then we would cook cornmeal porridge,
   Of which I'll share with you.
   My feet is my only carriage,
   So I've got to push on through,
   But while I'm gone...
   (Bridge)

On The Road Again

Words and Music by
Willie Nelson

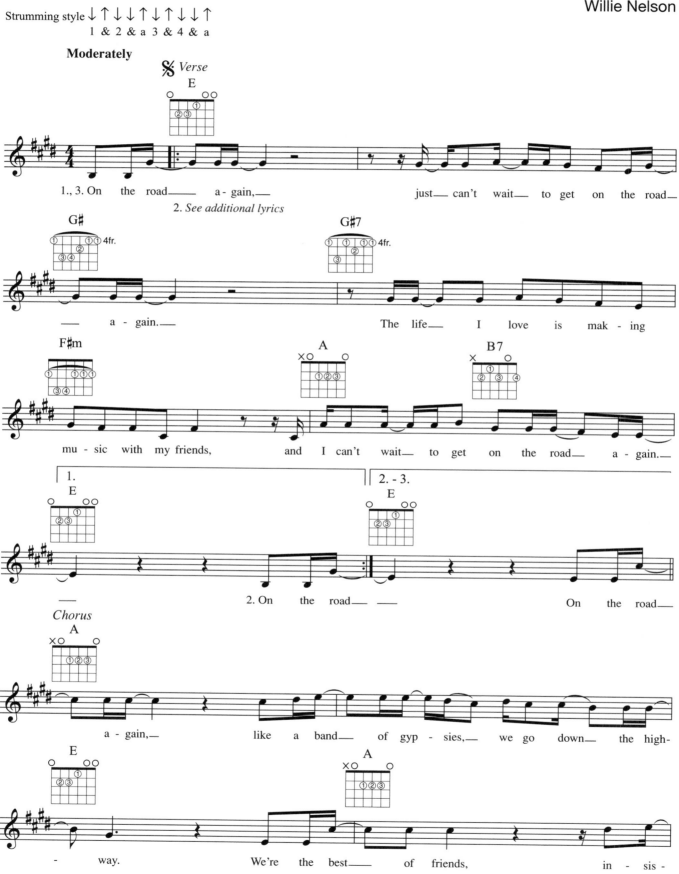

Additional lyrics

2. On the road again,
   Going places that I've never been,
   Seeing things that I may never see again,
   And I can't wait to get on the road again.

Open Arms

Words and Music by
Steve Perry and Jonathan Cain

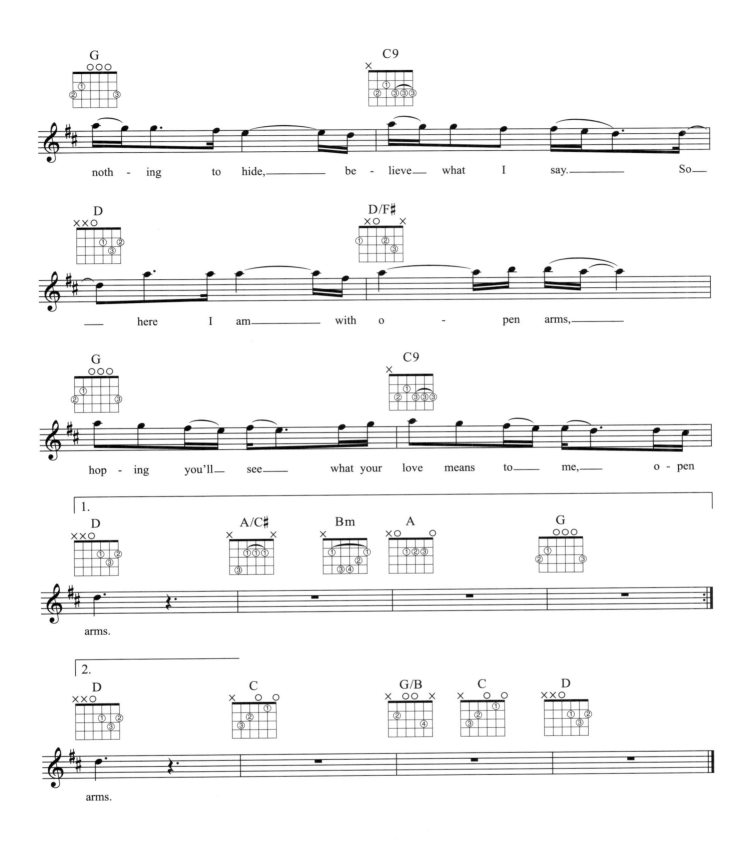

Additional lyrics

2. Living without you,
   Living alone,
   This empty house seems so cold,
   Wanting to hold you,
   Wanting you near,
   How much I wanted you home,
   But now that you've come back,
   Turned night into day,
   I need you to stay.

Redemption Song

Words and Music by
Bob Marley

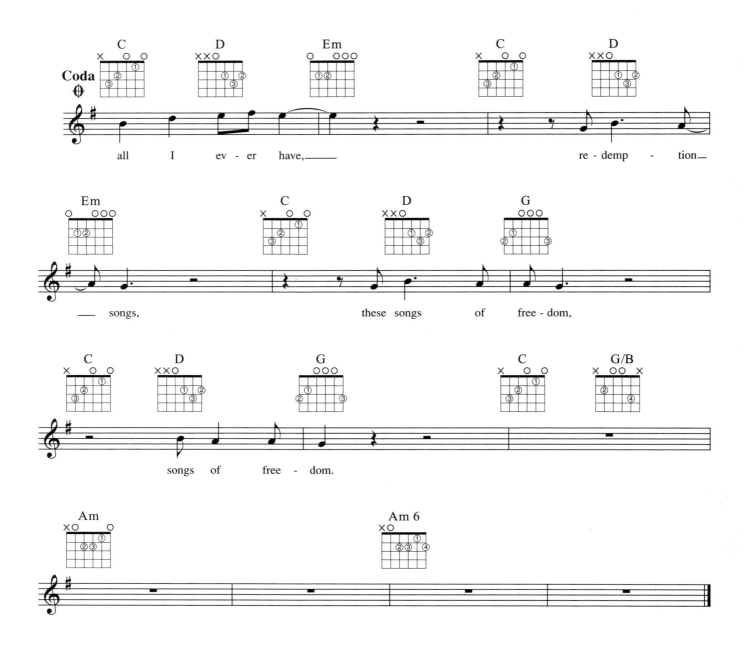

Additional lyrics

2., 3. Emancipate yourselves from mental slavery,
None but ourselves can free our minds.
Have no fear for atomic energy,
'Cos none of them can stop the time.
How long shall they kill our prophets,
While we stand aside and look?
Some say it's just a part of it,
We've got to fulfill the Book.

Raindrops Keep Fallin' On My Head

Words and Music by
Burt Bacharach and Hal David

Strumming style ↓ ↓ ↑ ↓ ↑ ↓ ↑ ↓ ↓ ↑ ↓ ↑ ↓ ↑

1 & a 2 a & a 3 & a 4 a & a

Moderate swing

1. Rain - drops keep fall - ing on my head and
2. *See additional lyrics*

just like the guy whose feet are too big for his

bed, noth - ing seems to fit, those rain - drops are fall - ing on my

1. head, they keep fall - ing_____ 2. So I just

2. But there's one

thing_____ I know,_____ the blues_____

they send — to meet — me won't de - feat — me, it

won't be long — 'til hap - pi - ness — steps up — to greet me. —

3. Rain drops keep fall - ing on my head but

that does - n't mean my eyes will soon be turn - ing red, cry - ing's not for

me, 'cos I'm nev - er gon - na stop the rain by com - plain - ing. —

to Coda

Be - cause I'm free, —

D.S. al Coda

Additional lyrics

2. So I just did me some talking to the sun,
   And I said I didn't like the way he got things done,
   Sleeping on the job.
   Those raindrops are falling on my head, they keep falling.

Say It Ain't So

Words and Music by
Rivers Cuomo

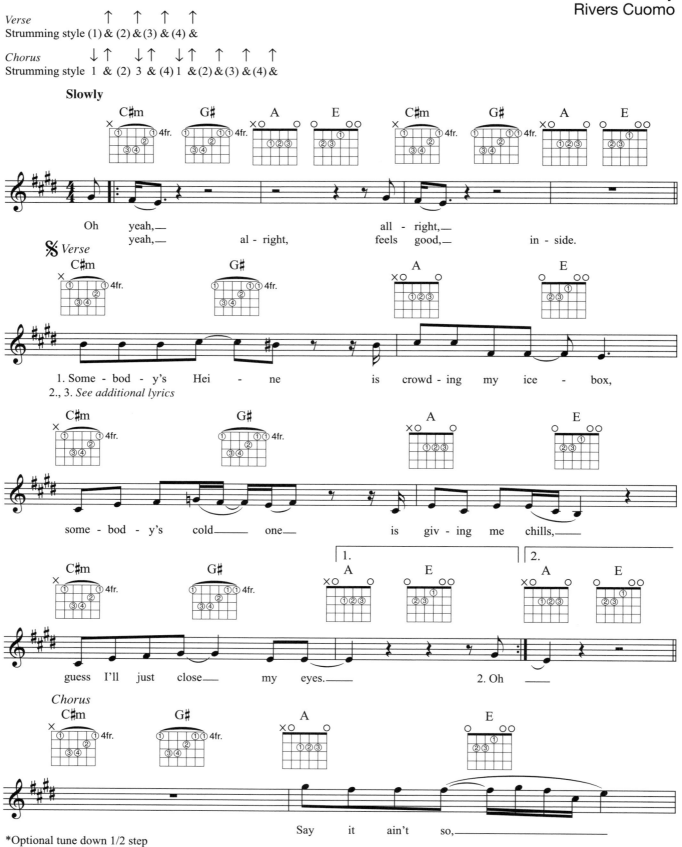

*Optional tune down 1/2 step

Additional lyrics

2. Oh, flip on the tele,
Wrestle with Jimmy,
Something is bubblin' behind my butt,
The bottle is ready to go.

3. I can't confront you,
I never could do
That which might hurt you,
To try and be cool,
When I say this way
Is a waterslide away from me
That takes you further everyday.
Be cool.

Santeria

Words and Music by
Brad Nowell, Eric Wilson and Floyd Gaugh

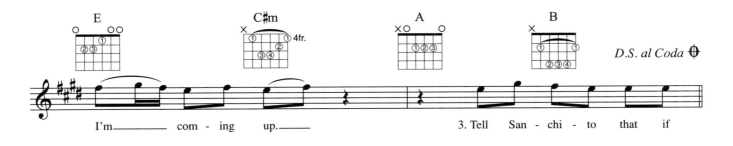

I'm—— com - ing up.—— 3. Tell San - chi - to that if

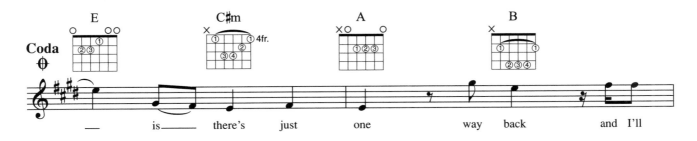

— is—— there's just one way back and I'll

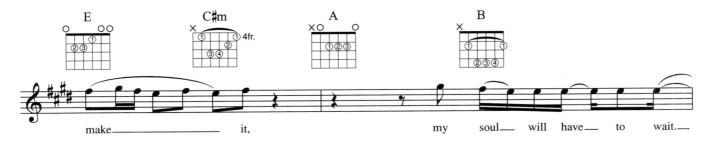

make——————— it, my soul— will have— to wait.——

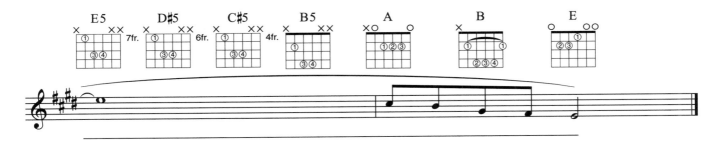

Additional lyrics

2. My soul will have to wait 'til I get back,
   Find heina of my own,
   Daddy's gonna love one and all.
   I feel the break,
   Feel the break,
   Feel the break and I got to live it up,
   Oh, yeah, huh, well I swear that I.

4. Tell Sanchito that if he knows what is good for him,
   He best go run and hide,
   Daddy's got a new .45,
   And I won't think twice to stick that barrel
   Straight down Sancho's throat,
   Believe me when I say,
   That I got somethin' for his punk ass.

Sister Golden Hair

Words and Music by
Gerry Beckley

Additional lyrics

2., 3. Well, I keep on thinking 'bout you,
Sister Golden Hair surprise,
And I just can't live without you,
Can't you see it in my eyes?
I've been one poor correspondent,
And I've been too, too hard to find,
But it doesn't mean you ain't been on my mind.

Soak Up The Sun

Words and Music by
Sheryl Crow and Jeff Trott

Strumming style ↓ ↓ ↓ ↑ ↓ ↑
            1 2 3 & 4 &

Moderately

1. My friend the com - mu - nist holds meet - ings in
2. *See additional lyrics*

— his R - V. I can't af - ford his gas,

1.
so I'm stuck here watch - ing T - V.

2.
— you've got.—

𝄋 *Chorus*

I'm gon - na soak up the sun,—

to Coda ⊕

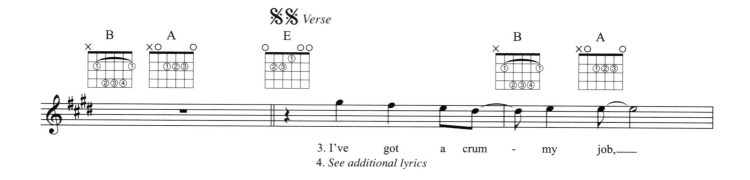

3. I've got a crum - my job,___
4. *See additional lyrics*

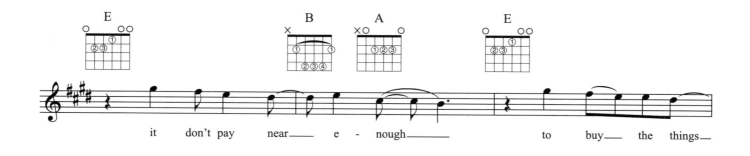

it don't pay near___ e - nough___ to buy___ the things___

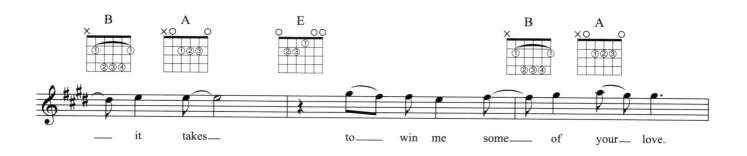

___ it takes___ to___ win me some___ of your___ love.

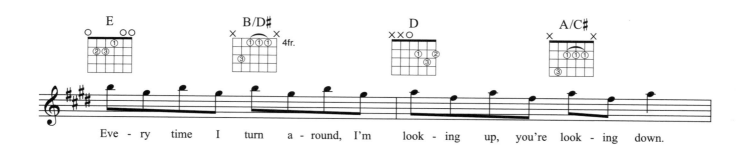

Eve - ry time I turn a - round, I'm look - ing up, you're look - ing down.

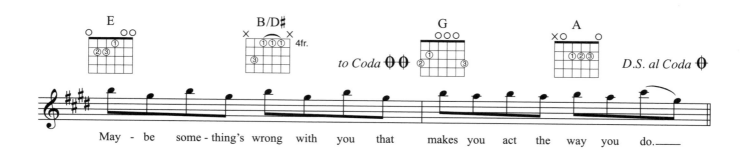

to Coda   *D.S. al Coda*

May - be some - thing's wrong with you that makes you act the way you do.___

got no one to blame,_____ but eve - ry time I feel

lame I'm_____ look - ing_____ up.

I,_____ I'm gon - na soak up the sun,_____

I've got my for - ty five on so_____ I can rock_____ on._____

Additional lyrics

2. I don't have digital,
   I don't have diddly-squat,
   It's not having what you want,
   It's wanting what you've got.

3. Don't have no master suite,
   I'm still the king of me.
   You have a fancy ride, but baby,
   I'm the one who has the key.
   Every time I turn around,
   I'm looking up, you're looking down,
   Maybe something's wrong with you,
   That makes you act the way you do.

Space Oddity

Words and Music by
David Bowie

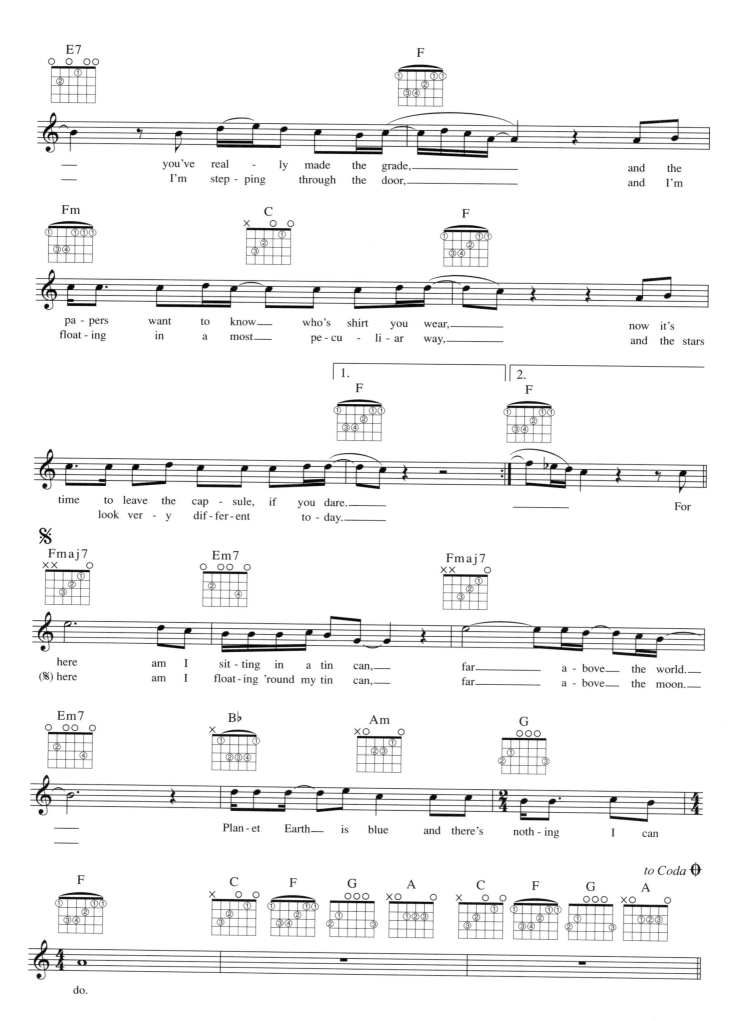

Spirit In The Sky

Words and Music by
Norman Greenbaum

Strumming style ↓ ↑ ↓ ↑ ↓ ↑ ↓ ↑

1 & 2 & 3 & 4 &

Moderate Swing

A

1. When I die and they lay me to rest,_____

2., 3. *See additional lyrics*

D

gon - na go_____ to the place_____ that's the best,_____

A

when they lay_____ me down_____ to die, go - ing up_____

E

_____ to the spir - it in the sky.

A

Go - ing up_____ to the spir - it in the sky,

D

it's where I'm gon - na go_____ when I die._____

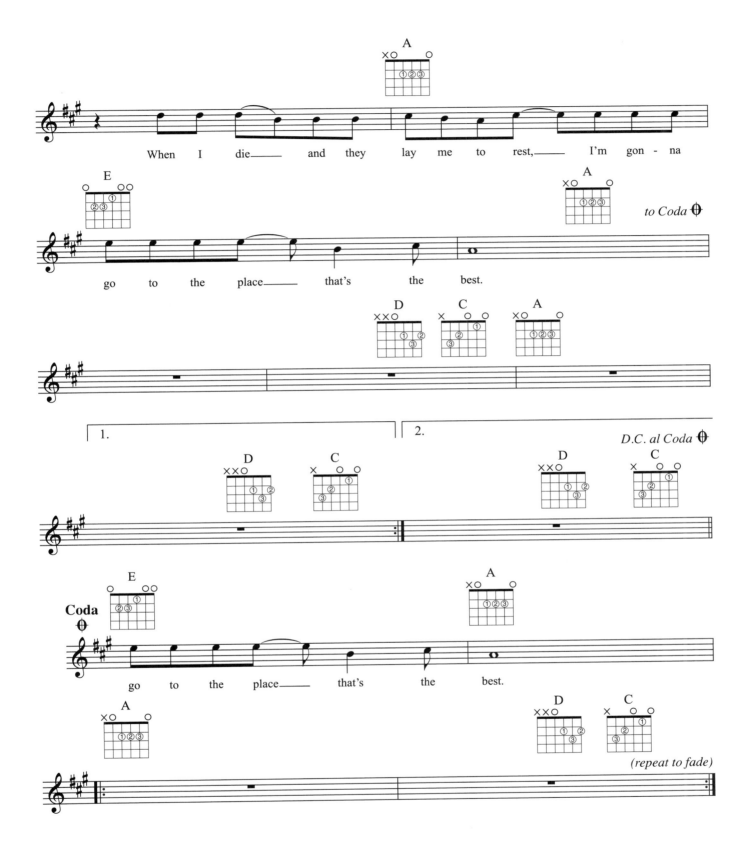

Additional lyrics

2. Prepare yourself, you know it's a must,
   Gotta have a friend in Jesus,
   So you know that when you die,
   He's gonna recommend you to the spirit in the sky.
   Whoa, recommend you to the spirit in the sky,
   That's where you're gonna go when you die,
   When you die and they lay you to rest,
   You're gonna go to the place that's the best.

3. Never been a sinner, I've never sinned,
   I've got a friend in Jesus,
   So you know that when I die,
   He's gonna set me up with the spirit in the sky.
   Whoa, set me up with the spirit in the sky,
   That's where I'm gonna go when I die,
   When I die and they lay me to rest,
   I'm gonna go to the place that's the best.

Stand By Me

Words and Music by
Jerry Leiber, Mike Stoller and Ben E. King

Strumming style ↓ ↓ ↑   ↑ ↓ ↑
1 2 & (3) & 4 &

Moderately

A

1. When the night_____ has come_____

2. See additional lyrics

F#m

and the land is_____ dark,_____ and the moon_____

D   E7

_____ is the on - ly_____ light we'll_____

A

see.   No I won't_____ be a - fraid,_____

F#m

_____ oh, I_____ won't   be a -

D

fraid,   just as   long_____   as   you stand,___

E 7   A

___   stand by_____ me.   So,   dar - lin',   dar - lin'

𝄋 *Chorus*

stand_____   by   me,_____   oh,_____   stand___

F♯m   D

_____   by   me,   oh,   stand,_____

E7   A

to Coda ⊕

stand   by_____   me.   stand   by_____   me.

| 1. | 2. |

D.S. al Coda ⊕

2. If   the   sky___ Dar - lin',   dar - lin'

Coda

by—— me.   When - ev - er you're in trou - ble won't you

stand———— by me,——— oh,———— stand——

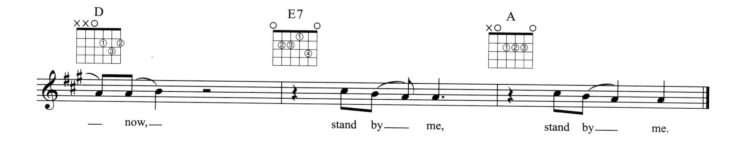

———— by—— me,——— whoa,—— stand——

— now,— stand by—— me, stand by—— me.

Additional lyrics

2. If the sky that we look upon,
   Should tumble and fall,
   Or the mountain should crumble to the sea,
   I won't cry, I won't cry, no I won't shed a tear,
   Just as long as you stand, stand by me.

Stuck In The Middle With You

Words and Music by
Gerry Rafferty and Joe Egan

Strumming style ↓ ↑ ↑ ↑ ↑
1 & (2) & (3) & (4) &

Moderately

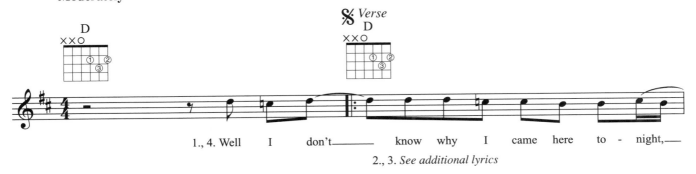

1., 4. Well I don't_____ know why I came here to - night,_____

2., 3. *See additional lyrics*

_____ I got the feel - ing that some - thing ain't right._____

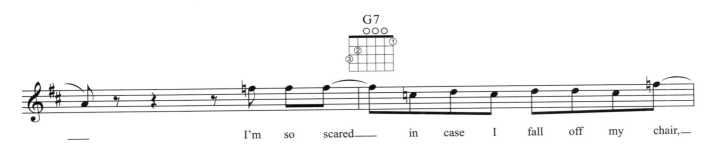

_____ I'm so scared_____ in case I fall off my chair,_____

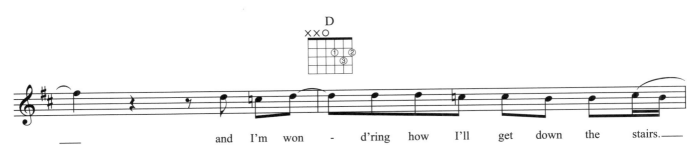

_____ and I'm won - d'ring how I'll get down the stairs._____

Chorus

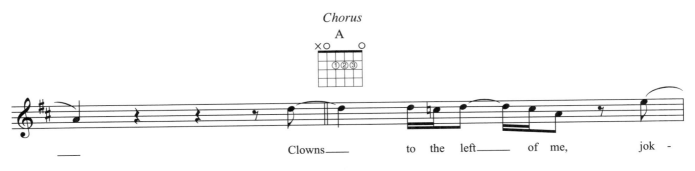

Clowns_____ to the left_____ of me, jok -

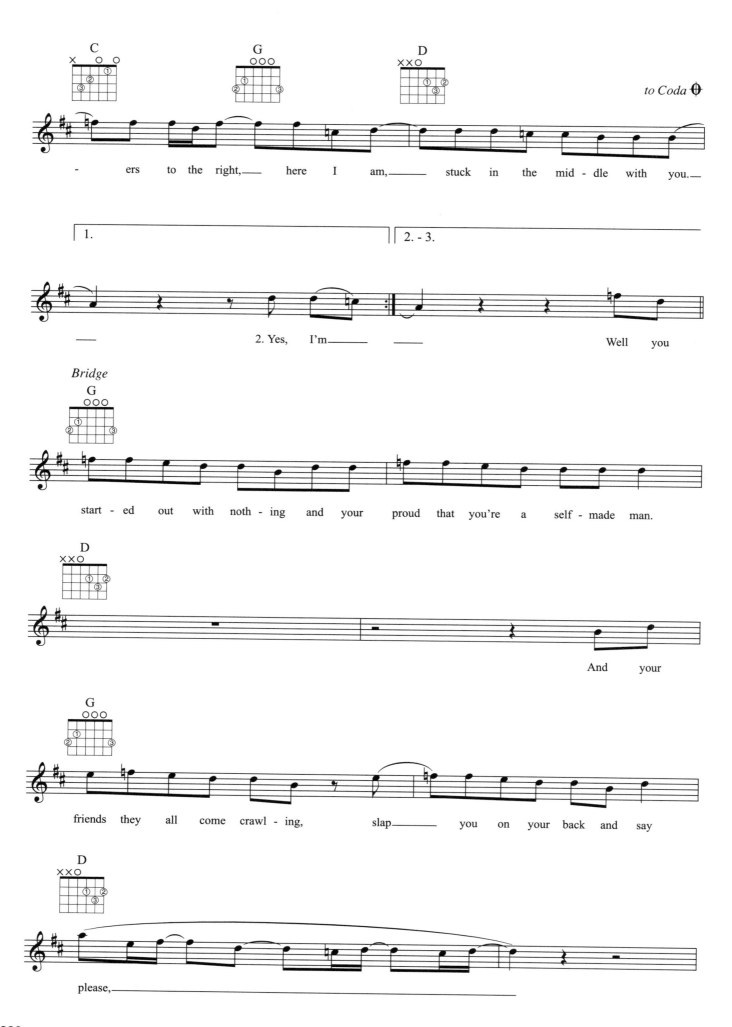

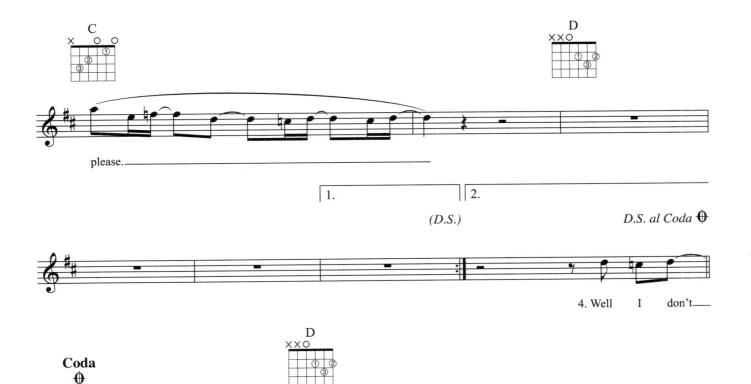

please.

1. *(D.S.)*

2. *D.S. al Coda*

4. Well I don't___

Coda

___ Yes, I'm___ stuck in the mid - dle with you,___

stuck in the mid - dle with you,___ yes, I'm___

___ stuck in the mid - dle with you.___

Additional lyrics

2. Yes, I'm stuck in the middle with you,
   And I'm wondering what it is I should do,
   It's so hard to keep this smile from my face,
   Losing control, yeah, I'm all over the place.
   (Chorus)

3. Tryin' to make some sense of it all,
   But I can see that it makes no sense at all.
   Is it cool to go to sleep on the floor?
   'Cos I don't think that I can take anymore.
   (Chorus)

Summertime Blues

Words and Music by
Eddie Cochran and Jerry Capehart

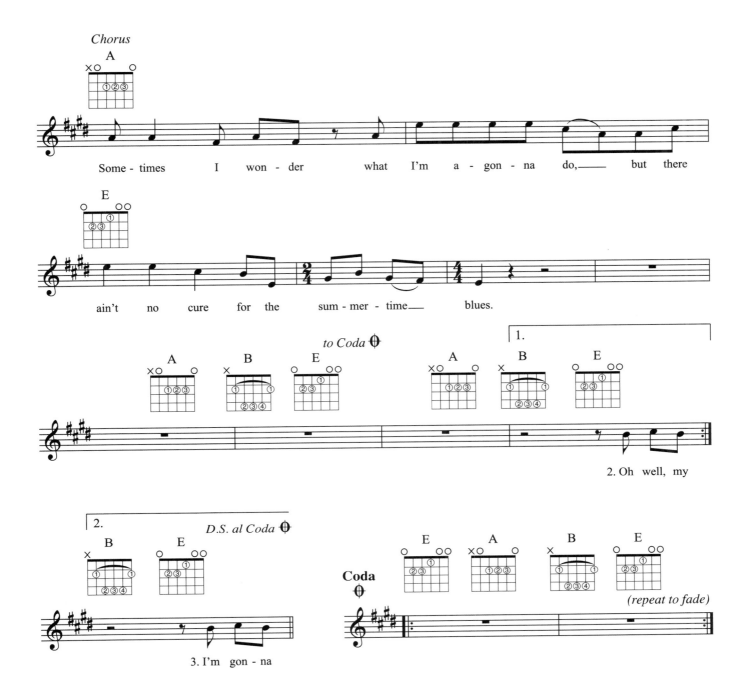

Additional lyrics

2. Oh well, my mom and poppa told me,
   "Son, you gotta make some money,
   If you wanna use the car
   To go a-ridin' next Sunday,"
   Well, I didn't go to work,
   Told the boss I was sick.
   "Now you can't use the car,
   'Cos you didn't work a lick."
   (Chorus)

3. I'm gonna take two weeks,
   Gonna have a fine vacation.
   I'm gonna take my problem
   To the United Nations.
   I called up my congressman,
   And he said, quote,
   "I'd like to help you son,
   But you're too young to vote."
   (Chorus)

Superstar

Words and Music by
Bonnie Sheridan and Leon Russell

Verse ↓ ↑↓↓↑
Strumming style 1(2) & 3 4 &

Chorus ↓↓↑↑↓↓↑↓↓↑↓↓↑
Strumming style 1 & a 2 & a 3 & a 4 & a

Moderately slow

Verse

Em   D   C   G/B

1. Long a - go_____ and oh, so_____ far a - way,_____ I fell in_____
2. *See additional lyrics*

A7   C   Bm

_____ love with you_____ be - fore the sec - ond show._____

Em   D

_____ Your gui - tar,_____ it sounds_____ so_____

C   G/B   A7

_____ sweet and clear_____ but you're_____ not_____ real - ly here,_____

C   Bm

_____ it's just the ra - di - o._____

Additional lyrics

2. Loneliness is such a sad affair,
And I can hardly wait
To be with you again.
What to say, to make you come again?
Come back to me again,
And play your sad guitar.

Take It On The Run

Words and Music by
Gary Richrath

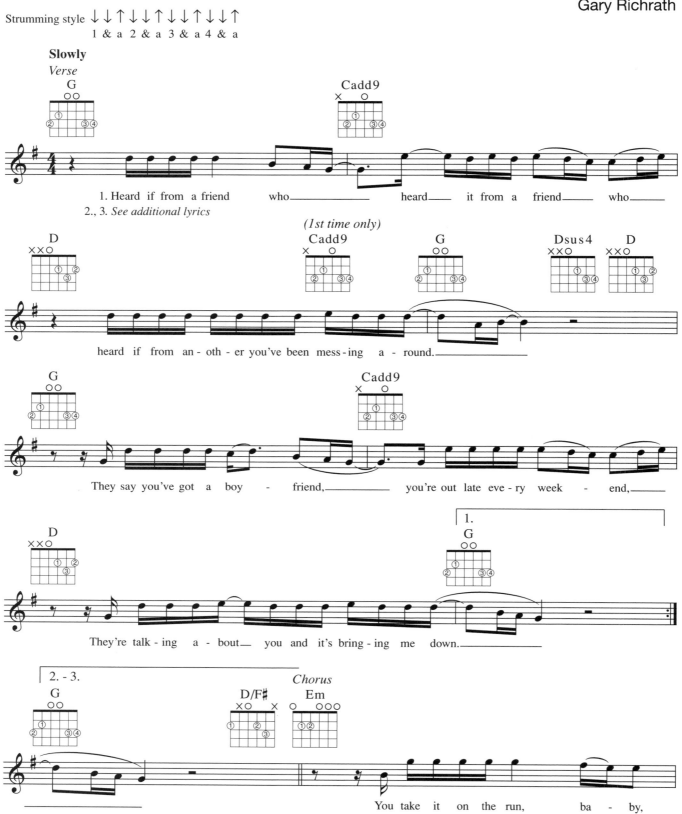

Strumming style ↓ ↓ ↑ ↓ ↓ ↑ ↓ ↓ ↑ ↓ ↓ ↑

1 & a 2 & a 3 & a 4 & a

Slowly

Verse

G   Cadd9

1. Heard if from a friend   who_____   heard___ it from a friend___ who___
2., 3. *See additional lyrics*

D   *(1st time only)*   Cadd9   G   Dsus4   D

heard if from an-oth-er you've been mess-ing a-round.___

G   Cadd9

They say you've got a boy - friend,_____ you're out late eve-ry week - end,___

D   1.
                                                    G

They're talk-ing a-bout___ you and it's bring-ing me down.___

2. - 3.   *Chorus*
G   D/F♯   Em

You take it on the run, ba - by,

Additional lyrics

2. But I know the neighborhood,
   And talk is cheap when the story is good,
   And the tales grow taller on down the line.
   But I'm telling you, babe,
   That I don't think it's true, babe,
   And even if it is keep this in mind.
   (Chorus)

3. You're thinking up your white lies,
   You're putting on your bedroom eyes,
   You say you're coming home,
   But you won't say when.
   But I can feel it coming,
   If you leave tonight, keep running,
   And you need never look back again.
   (Chorus)

There Is No Greater Love

Words and Music by
Marty Symes and Isham Jones

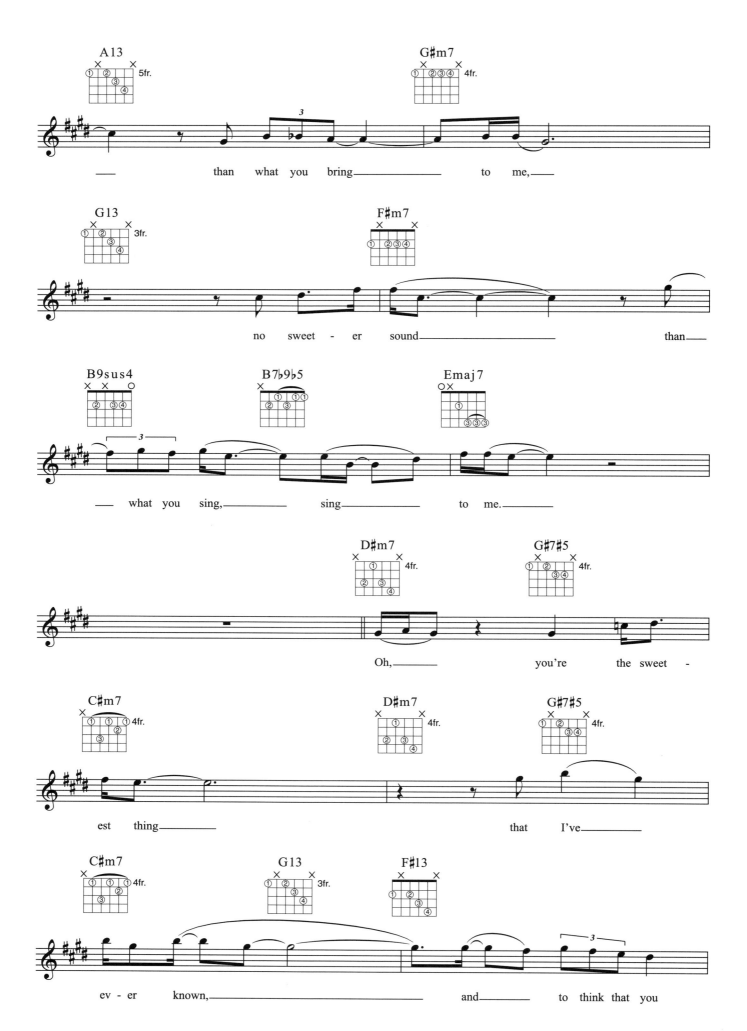

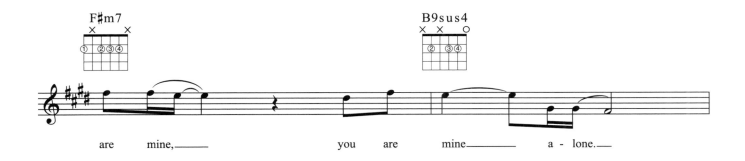

are mine,_____ you are mine_____ a - lone._____

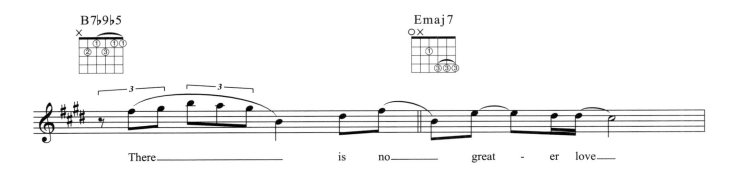

There_____ is no_____ great - er love_____

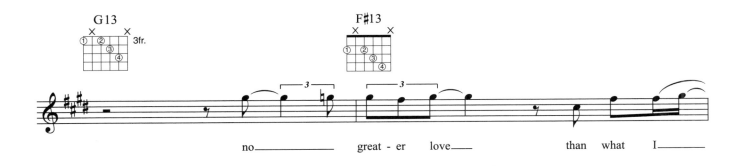

in all the world, it's true,____

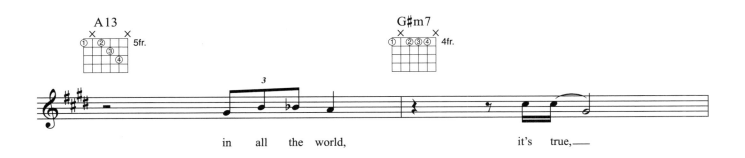

no_____ great - er love_____ than what I_____

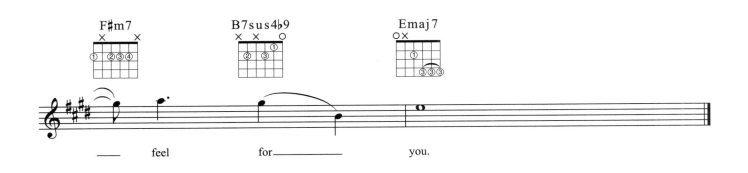

____ feel for_____ you.

These Boots Are Made For Walkin'

Words and Music by
Lee Hazlewood

Strumming style ↓ ↓ ↑ ↓ ↓ ↑ ↓ ↓ ↑ ↓ ↓ ↑

1 & a 2 & a 3 & a 4 & a

Fast swing

1. You keep say-ing you've got some-thing for——— me,

2., 3. *See additional lyrics*

some-thing you call love, but con - fess.

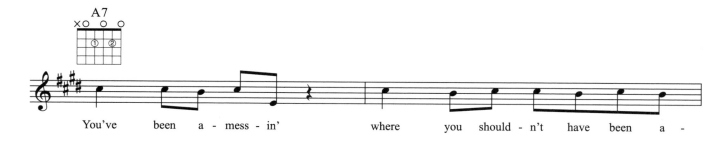

You've been a - mess - in' where you should - n't have been a -

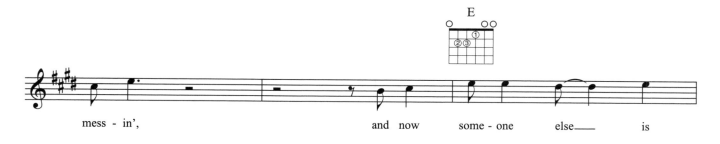

mess - in', and now some - one else——— is

get - ting all——— your best.——— These

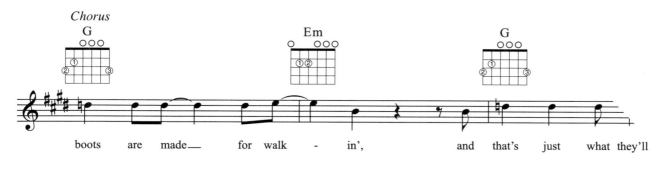

Chorus

boots are made— for walk - in', and that's just what they'll

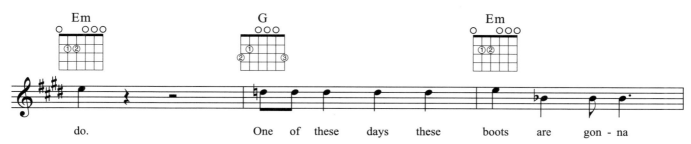

do. One of these days these boots are gon - na

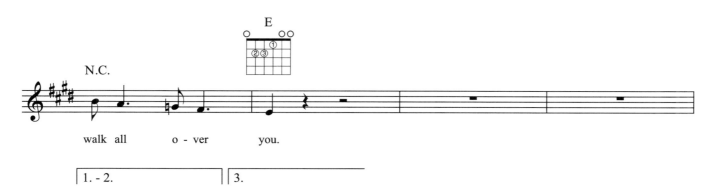

walk all o - ver you.

| 1. - 2. | 3. |

Are you read - y, boots?

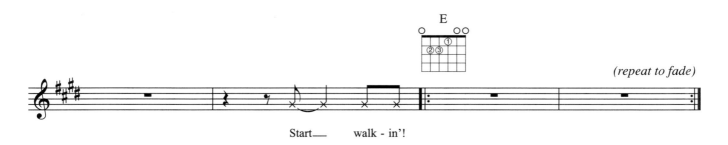

(repeat to fade)

Start— walk - in'!

Additional lyrics

2. You keep lyin' when you oughta be truthin',
And you keep losin' when you oughta not bet.
You keep samin' when you oughta be a-changin'.
Now what's right is right but you ain't been right yet.
(Chorus)

3. You keep playin' where you shouldn't be playin',
And you keep thinkin' that you'll never get burnt.
I just found me a brand new box of matches, yeah,
And what he know you ain't had time to learn.
(Chorus)

Total Eclipse Of The Heart

Words and Music by
Jim Steinman

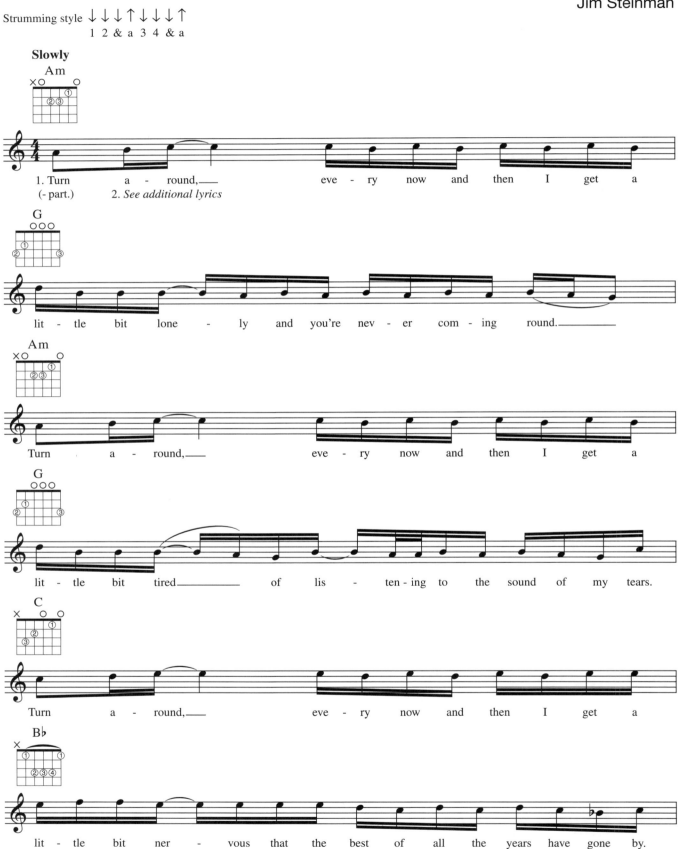

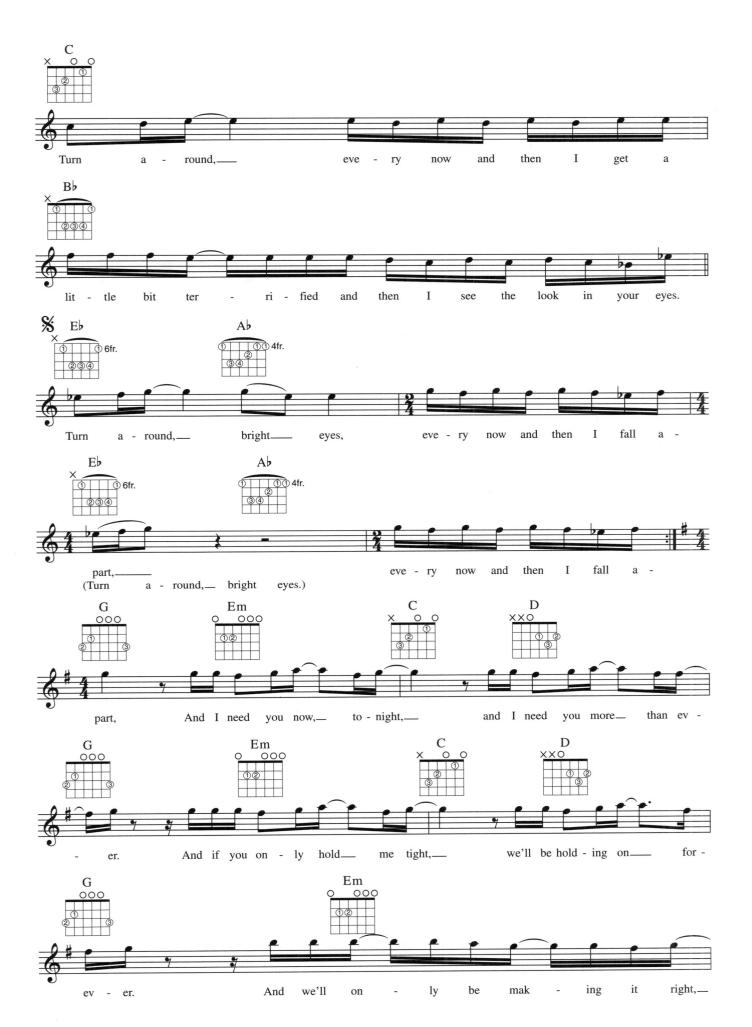

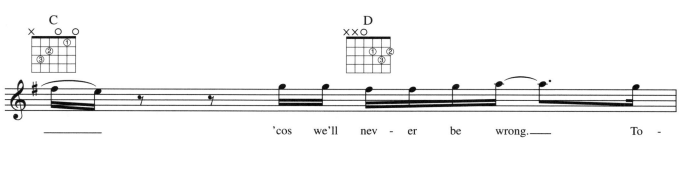

'cos we'll nev-er be wrong.___ To -

geth-er we can take it to the end of the line,___ your love is like a shad-ow on me

all of the time._____ I

to Coda ⊕

don't know what to do and I'm al - ways in the dark,___ we're liv-ing in a pow-der keg and

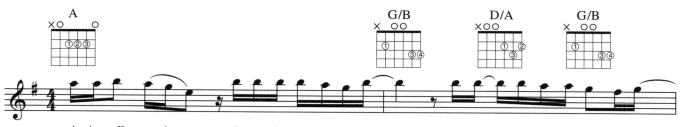

giv-ing off sparks.___ I real-ly need you to-night,___ for-ev - er's gon-na start to-night,___

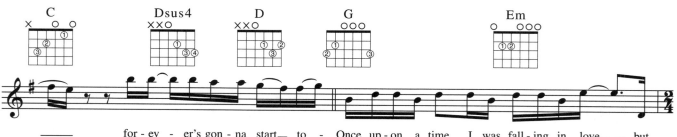

___ for-ev-er's gon-na start___ to - Once up-on a time I was fall-ing in love,___ but
(- night.)

now I'm on - ly fall - ing a - part,_____ there's

noth - ing I can do, a to - tal e - clipse___ of the heart.___

Once up - on a time there was light in my life,___ but

now there's on - ly love in the dark,_____

noth - ing I can say, a to - tal e - clipse___ of the heart.___

D.S. (no repeat) al Coda

Coda

giv - ing off sparks.___ I real - ly need you to - night,___

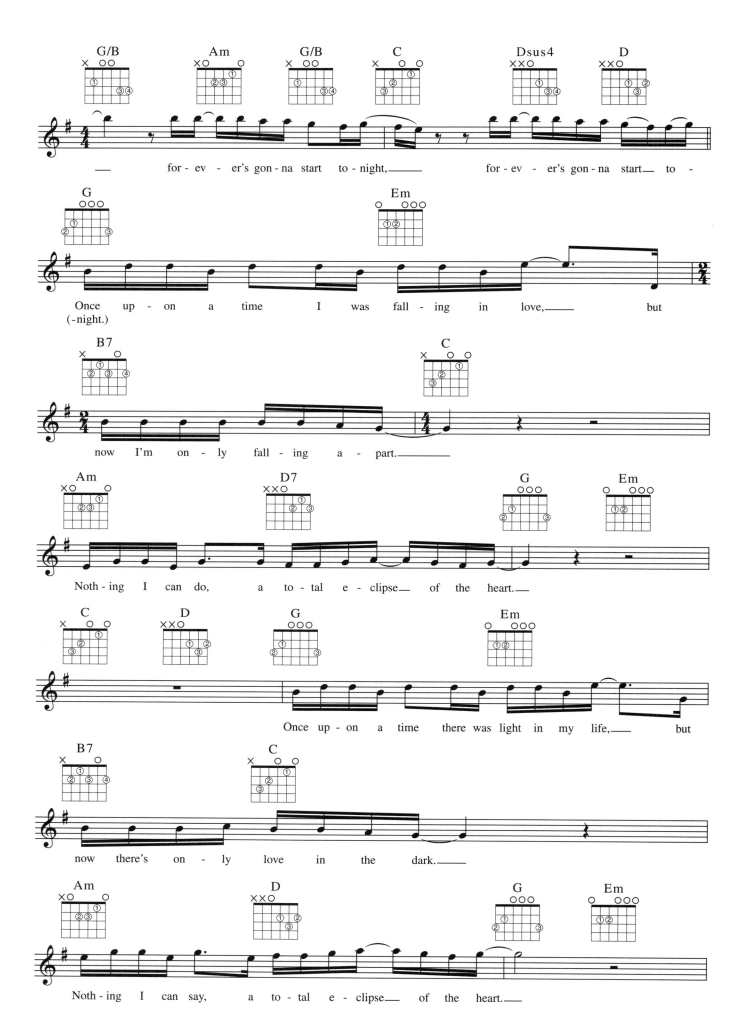

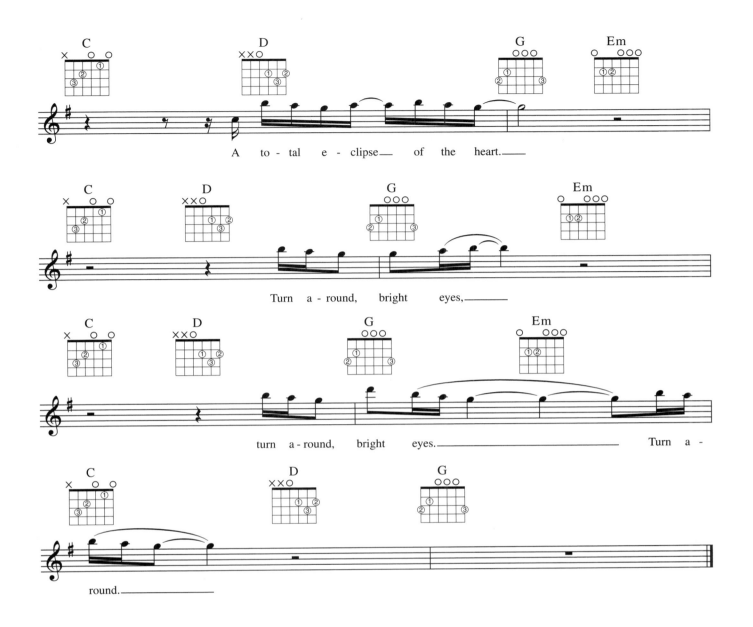

Additional lyrics

2. Turn around. Every now and then
   I get a little bit restless and I dream of something wild.
   Turn around. Every now and then
   I get a little bit helpless and I'm lying like a child in your arms.
   Turn around. Every now and then
   I get a little bit angry and I know I've got to get out and cry.
   Turn around. Every now and then
   I get a little bit terrified but then I see the look in your eyes.
   Turn around bright eyes.
   Every now and then I fall apart.
   Turn around bright eyes.
   Every now and then I fall apart.

Unchain My Heart

Words and Music by
Bobby Sharp and Teddy Powell

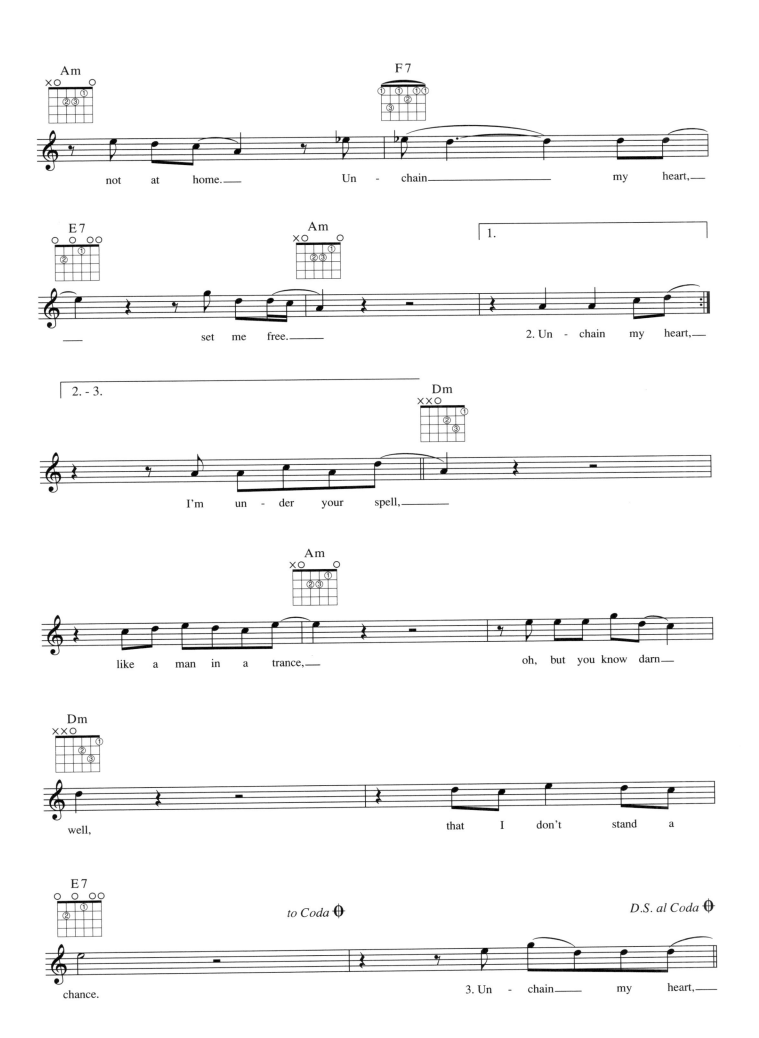

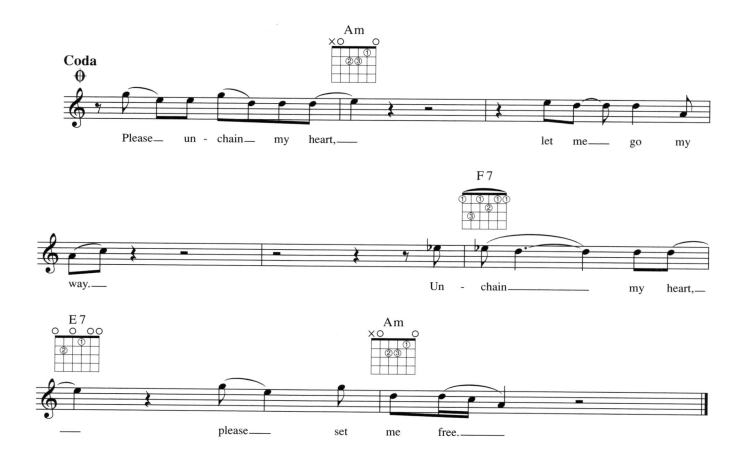

Coda

Please— un - chain— my heart,—— let me— go my way.—— Un - chain—————— my heart,— —— please—— set me free.————

Additional lyrics

2. Unchain my heart,
   Baby, let me be.
   Unchain my heart,
   'Cos you don't care about me.
   You got me sewed up like a pillow case,
   But you let my love go to waste.
   Unchain my heart, set me free.

3. Unchain my heart,
   Let me go my way.
   Unchain my heart,
   You worry me night and day.
   Why lead me through a life of misery.
   When you don't care a bag of beans for me?
   Unchain my heart, set me free.

Ventura Highway

Words and Music by
Dewey Bunnell

Strumming style ↓ ↓ ↓ ↑ ↓ ↑ ↓ ↑

1 2 & a 3 & 4 &

Moderately

Verse

G6

1. Chew - ing on a piece of grass, walk - ing down the road,
2. *See additional lyrics*

Dmaj7   **G6**

Tell me how long you gon - na stay here, Joe?

Dmaj7

G6

Some peo - ple say, this town don't look good in snow. You don't

Dmaj7   **G6**

Dmaj7

care, I know.

(repeat to fade)

Additional lyrics

2. Wishing on a falling star,
Waiting for the early train.
Sorry boy, but I've been hit by purple rain.
Aw, come on Joe, you can always change your name,
"Thanks a lot son, just the same."

Up On Cripple Creek

Words and Music by
Robbie Robertson

Strumming style ↓ ↓ ↑ ↓ ↓ ↑ ↓ ↓ ↑ ↓ ↓ ↑

1 & a 2 & a 3 & a 4 & a

Slowly

Verse

A   D

1. When I get off of this moun-tain, you know where I wan-na go,
2. - 5. *See additional lyrics*

A   D   E

straight down the Mis-sis-sip-pi Riv-er to the Gulf of Mex-i-co. To

A   D

Lake Charles, Lou-i-si-an-a, Lit-tle Bes-sie girl I once knew,

A   D   E

she told me just to come on by, if there's an-y-thing she could do.

Chorus

A   D

Up on Crip-ple Creek, she sends me, if I spring a leak, she mends me,

I don't have_____ to speak, she de-fends_____ me, a

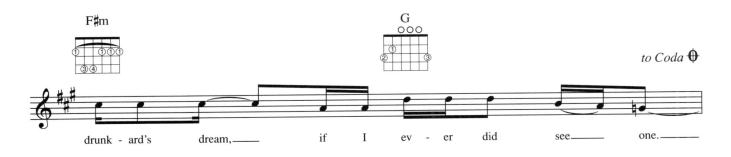

drunk - ard's dream,_____ if I ev - er did see_____ one._____

1. - 3.   **4. - 5.**   *Bridge*

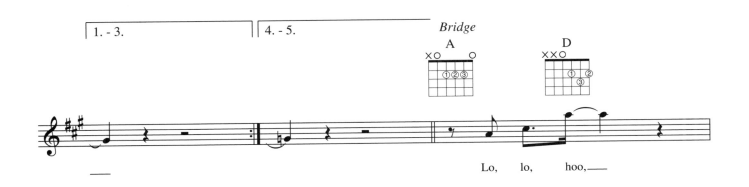

Lo, lo, hoo,_____

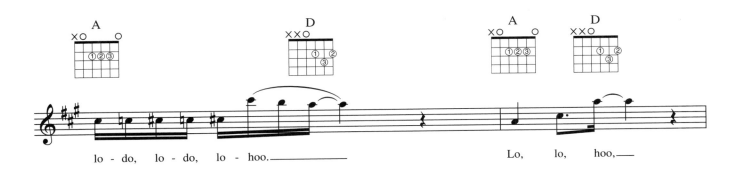

lo - do, lo - do, lo - hoo._____   Lo, lo, hoo,_____

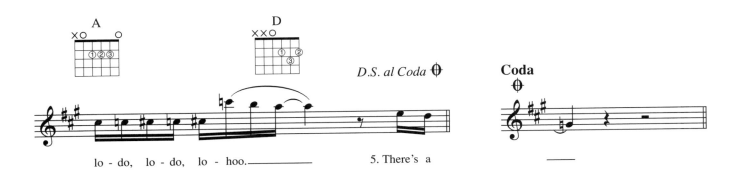

D.S. al Coda   **Coda**

lo - do, lo - do, lo - hoo._____   5. There's a   _____

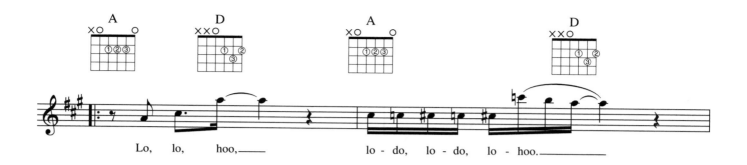

Lo, lo, hoo,—— lo - do, lo - do, lo - hoo.——

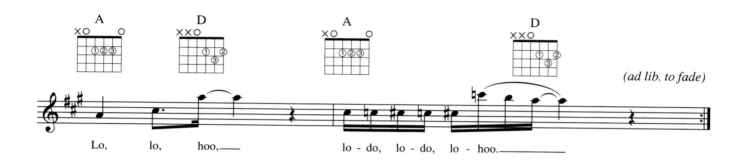

(ad lib. to fade)

Lo, lo, hoo,—— lo - do, lo - do, lo - hoo.——

Additional lyrics

2. Good luck had just stung me,
   To the race track I did go.
   She bet on one horse to win,
   And I bet on another to show.
   Odds were in my favor,
   I had him five to one.
   When that nag to win came around the track,
   Sure enough he had won.

3. I took up all of my winnings,
   And I gave my little Bessie half.
   And she tore it up and threw it in my face,
   Just for a laugh.
   Now there's one thing in the whole, wide world
   I sure do like to see.
   That's when that little love of mine
   Dips her donut in my tea.

4. Now me and my mate were back at the shack,
   We had Spike Jones on the box.
   She said, "I can't take the way he sings,
   But I love to hear him talk."
   Now that just gave my heart a fall,
   To the bottom of my feet,
   And I swore as I took another pour,
   My Bessie can't be beat.

5. There's a flood out in California,
   And up north it's freezing cold,
   And this living off the road
   Is getting pretty old.
   So I guess I'll call up my big Mama,
   Tell her I'll be rolling in.
   But you know, deep down, I'm kinda tempted
   To go and see my Bessie again.

Wild Horses

Words and Music by
Mick Jagger and Keith Richards

Strumming style ↓ ↑ ↓ ↑ ↓ ↑ ↓ ↑
1 & 2 (&) a 3 & 4 &

Slowly

Verse

Bm   **G**

1. Child - hood liv - ing

2., 3. *See additional lyrics*

Bm   **G**

is eas - y to do. _____

Am7   **G** **C**   **D**

The things_____ you_____ want - ed,_____

G   **D**   **C**

I bought_____ them_____ for you.

Bm   **G**

Grace - less la - dy_____

you know_____ who I am._____

You know___ I can't_____ let___ you_____

Chorus

slide through my hands._____ Wild_____

_____ hors - es_____ could - n't drag me___ a -

way.___ Wild,___ wild___ hors - es_____

1. - 2.

could - n't drag me_____ a - way.___

Additional lyrics

2. I watched you suffer a dull, aching pain.
   Now you decided to show me the same.
   No sweeping exits or offstage lines
   Could make me feel bitter or treat you unkind.

3. I know I dreamed you a sin and a lie.
   I have my freedom but I don't have much time.
   Faith has been broken, tears must be cried.
   Let's do some living after we die.

The Weight

Words and Music by
J.R. Robertson

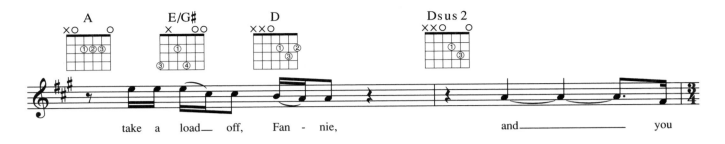

take a load off, Fan - nie, and_____ you

1. - 3.

to Coda

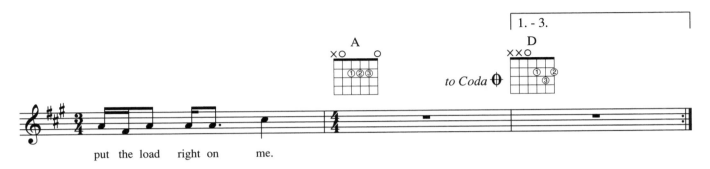

put the load right on me.

4.

D.C. al Coda

Coda

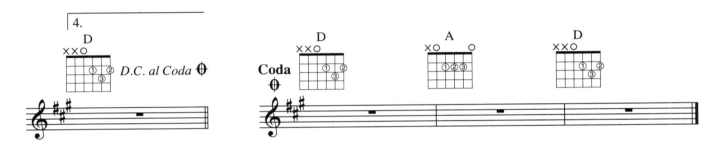

Additional lyrics

2. I picked up my bag, I went looking for a place to hide,
   When I saw Carmen and the Devil walkin' side by side.
   I said, "Hey, Carmen, come on, let's go downtown."
   She said, "I gotta go, but my friend can stick around."

3. Go down, Miss Moses, there's nothing you can say,
   It's just ol' Luke, and Luke's waitin' on the Judgement Day.
   "Well, Luke, my friend, what about young Anna Lee?"
   He said, "Do me a favor, son,
   Won't you stay and keep Anna Lee company?"

4. Crazy Chester followed me and he caught me in the fog.
   He said, "I will fix your rags, if you'll take Jack, my dog."
   I said, "Wait a minute, Chester, you know I'm a peaceful man."
   He said, "That's okay, boy, won't you feed him when you can?"

5. Catch a Cannonball, now, to take me down the line.
   My bag is sinking low and I do believe it's time
   To get back to Miss Fannie,
   You know she's the only one
   Who sent me here with her regards for everyone.

Whiskey In The Jar

Words and Music by
Philip Parris Lynott, Brian Michael Downey and Eric Bell

Strumming style ↓ ↑ ↓ ↑ ↓ ↑ ↓ ↑
1 & 2 & 3 & 4 &

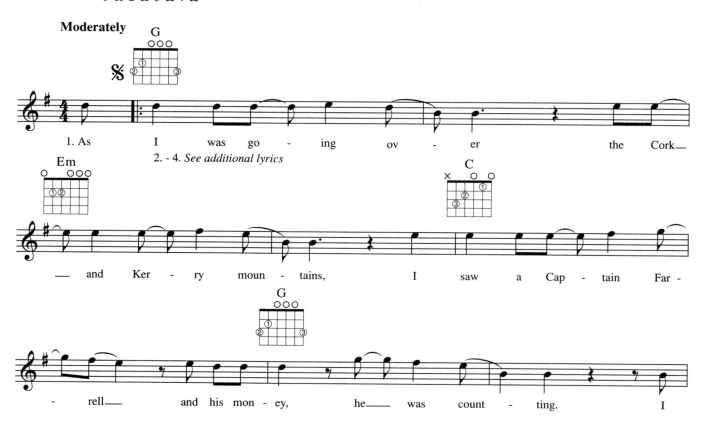

1. As I was go - ing ov - er the Cork—

2. - 4. *See additional lyrics*

— and Ker - ry moun - tains, I saw a Cap - tain Far -

- rell— and his mon - ey, he— was count - ing. I

first pro - duced— my pis - tol and then—

— pro - duced— my ra - pi - er. I said,—

"Stand and— de - liv - er, or the Dev - il, he— may take—

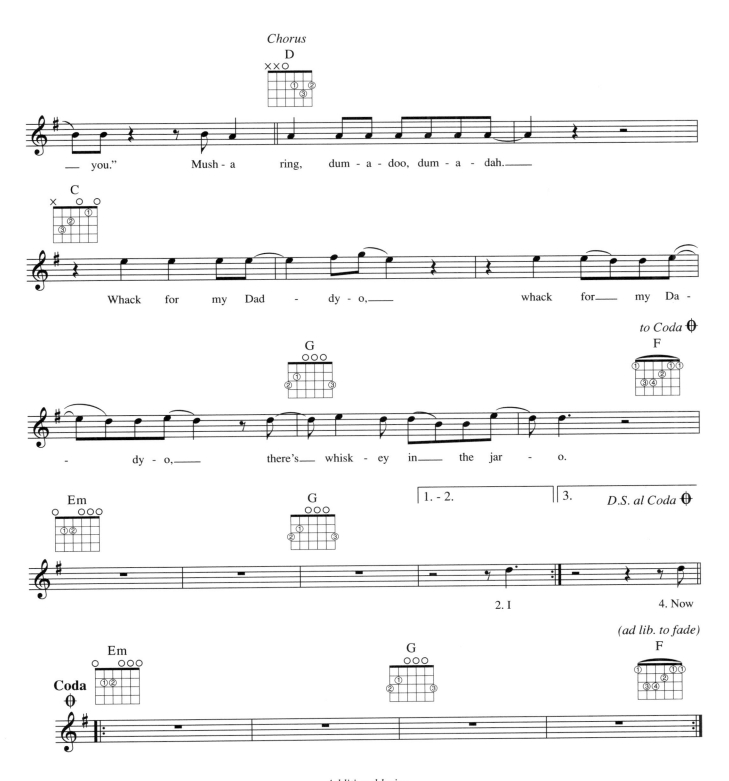

Additional lyrics

2. I took all of his money, and it was a pretty penny.
   I took all of his money and I brought it home to Molly.
   She swore that she'd love me, never would she leave me.
   But the devil take that woman, for you know she tricked me easy.

3. Being drunk and weary, I went to Molly's chamber,
   Taking my money with me, and I never knew the danger.
   For about six or maybe seven, in walked Captain Farrell.
   I jumped up, fired off my pistols, and I shot him with both barrels.

4. Now some men like the fishin' and some men like the fowlin',
   And some men like ta hear a cannon ball a-roarin',
   Me, I like sleepin', 'specially in my Molly's chamber,
   But here I am in prison, here I am with a ball and chain, yeah.

You Can't Always Get What You Want

Words and Music by
Mick Jagger and Keith Richards

Strumming style

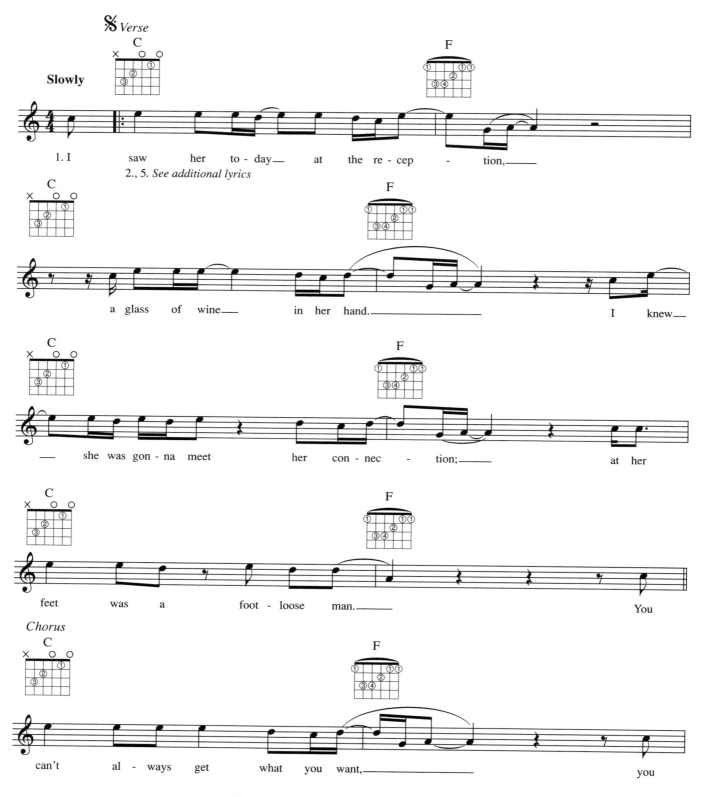

can't al - ways get what you want,_____ you

can't al - ways get what you want,_____ but if you

try some - times,_____ you might__ find_____ you get what you

need.__   2. And I

2. Verse

3. I went down_____ to the Chel - sea drug -
4. *See additional lyrics*

- store_____ to get__ your__ pre - scrip - tion filled.__ I was

stand - ing in line__ with Mis - ter Jim - my,_____ and man,__

did he look pret-ty ill.   4. We de-cid -   I said to him, you

Chorus

can't al-ways get what you want,   you

can't al-ways get what you want,   you

can't al-ways get what you want,   but if you

try some-times,   you might find   you get what you

D.S. al Coda

need.

5. I

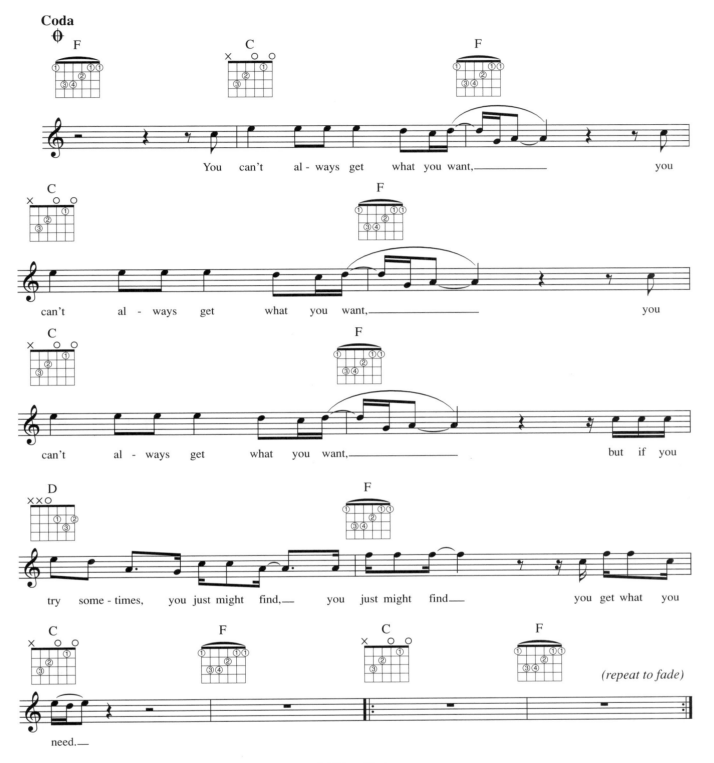

Additional lyrics

2. And I went down to the demonstration
   To get my fair share of abuse,
   Singing, "We're gonna vent our frustration.
   If we don't we're gonna blow a 50-amp fuse."
   Sing it to me now...
   (Chorus)

4. We decided that we would have a soda,
   My favorite flavor, cherry red.
   I sung my song to Mister Jimmy,
   Yeah, and he said one word to me, and that was "dead."
   I said to him...
   (Chorus)

5. I saw her today at the reception,
   In her glass was a bleeding man.
   She was practiced at the art of deception.
   Well, I could tell by her blood-stained hands.
   (Chorus)

You Shook Me All Night Long

Words and Music by
Angus Young, Malcolm Young and Brian Johnson

Strumming style ↓ ↓ ↓ ↑ ↓ ↑
1 2 3 & 4 &

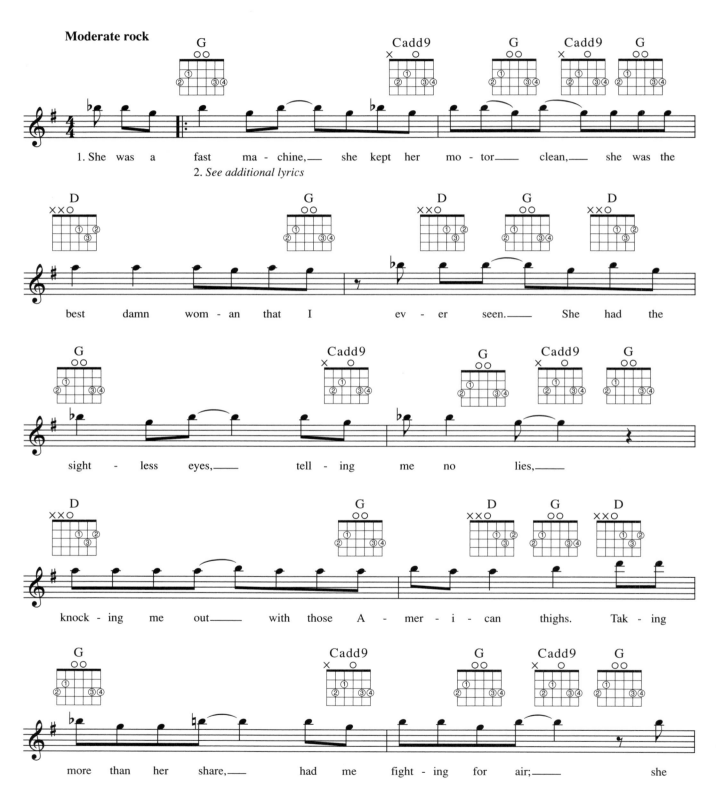

Moderate rock

1. She was a fast ma - chine,___ she kept her mo - tor___ clean,___ she was the
2. *See additional lyrics*

best damn wom - an that I ev - er seen.___ She had the

sight - less eyes,___ tell - ing me no lies,___

knock - ing me out___ with those A - mer - i - can thighs. Tak - ing

more than her share,___ had me fight - ing for air;___ she

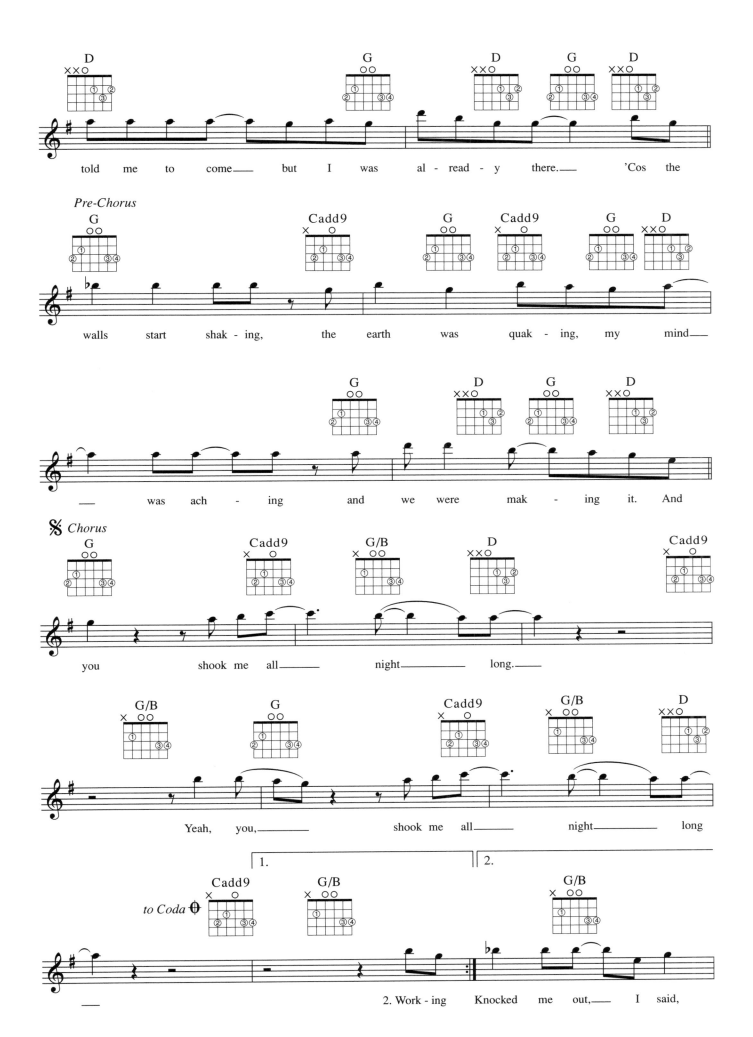

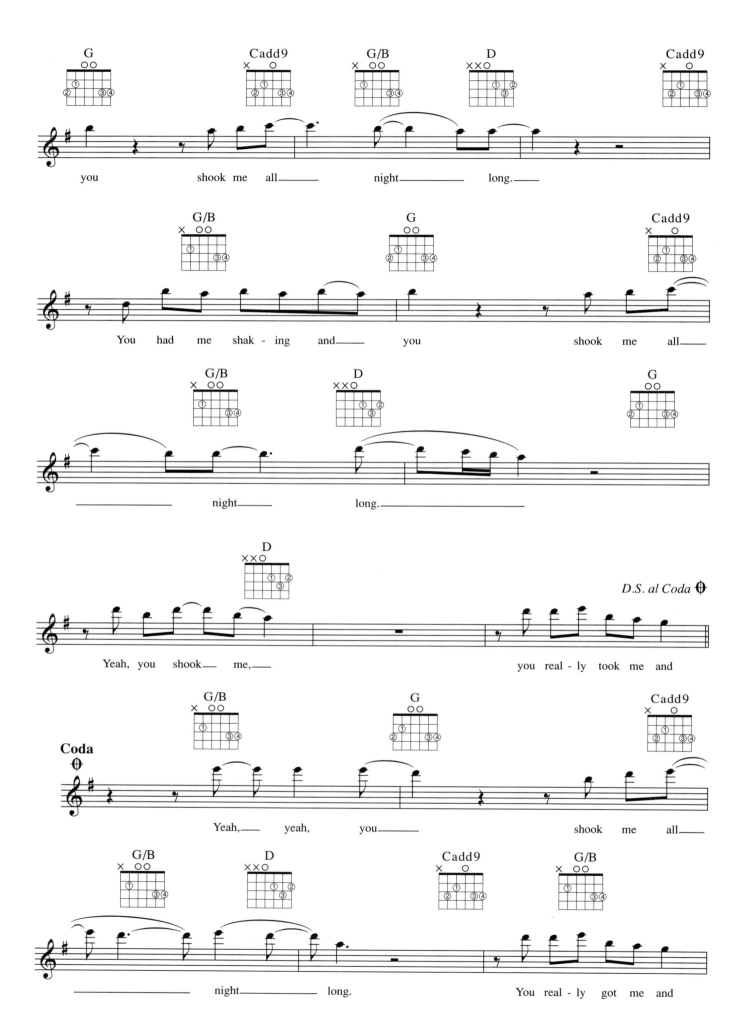

D.S. al Coda

Coda

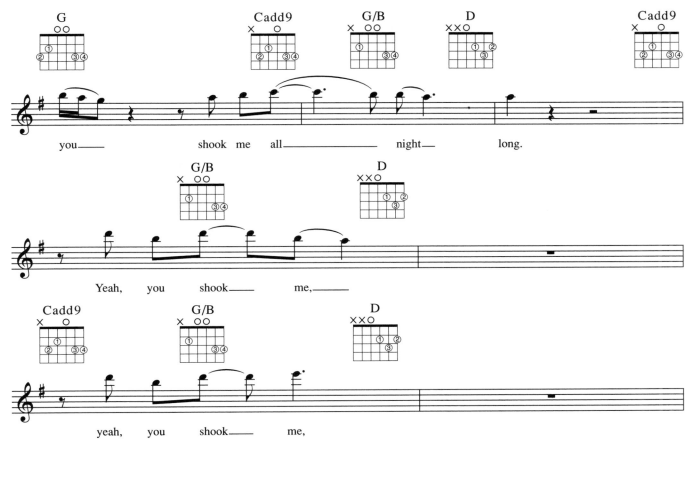

you_____ shook me all_____ night_____ long.

Yeah, you shook_____ me,_____

yeah, you shook_____ me,

all_____ night long._____

Additional lyrics

2. Working double-time on the seduction line,
   She was one of a kind, she's just mine, all mine.
   Wanted no applause, just another course;
   Made a meal out of me and come back for more.
   Had to cool me down to take another round,
   Now I'm back in the ring to take another swing.
   (Pre-Chorus)

Won't Get Fooled Again

Words and Music by
Pete Townshend

Strumming style ↓ ↓ ↑ ↓ ↑ ↓ ↑

1 2 & 3 & 4 &

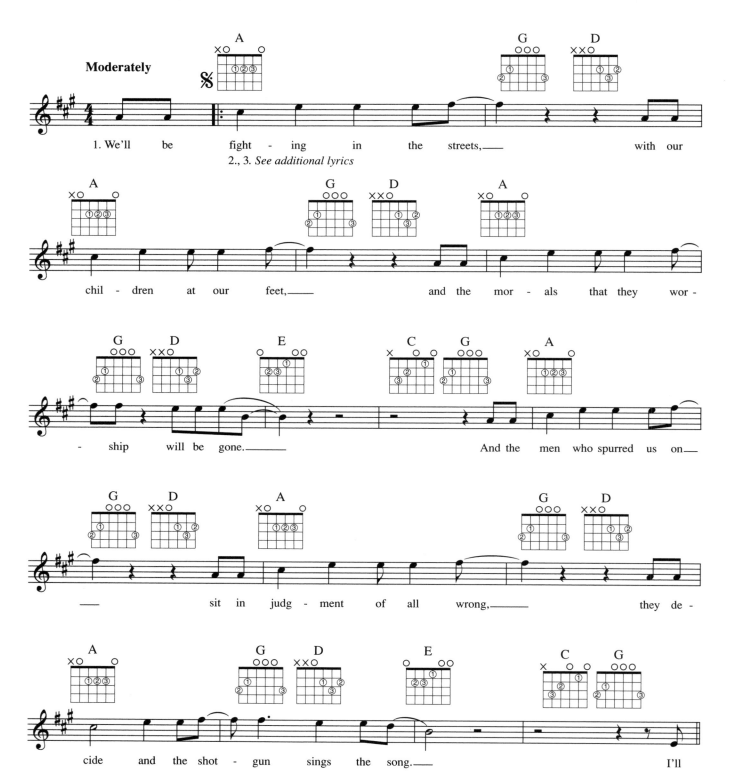

Moderately

1. We'll be fight-ing in the streets,_____ with our

2., 3. *See additional lyrics*

chil-dren at our feet,_____ and the mor-als that they wor-

-ship will be gone._____ And the men who spurred us on___

___ sit in judg-ment of all wrong,_____ they de-

cide and the shot-gun sings the song._____ I'll

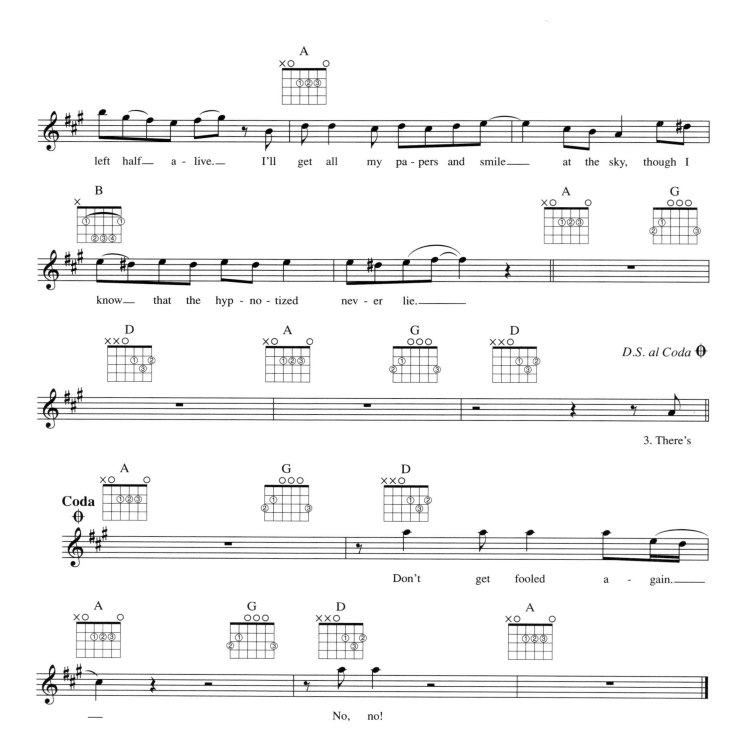

Additional lyrics

2. The change, it had to come,
   We knew it all along,
   We were liberated from the fold, that's all.
   And the world looks just the same,
   And history ain't changed,
   'Cos the banners, they all flown in the last war.
   (Chorus)

3. There's nothing in the street
   Looks any different to me,
   And the slogans are replaced, by the bye.
   And the parting on the left
   Is now a parting on the right,
   And the beards have all grown longer overnight.
   (Chorus)